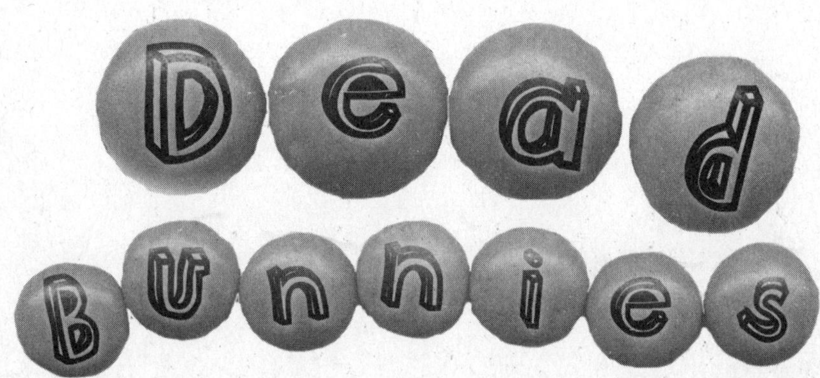

Because every life is a story God tells

Bryan Currie

Franklin, TN

Ninny Publishing
Post Office Box 682882 | Franklin, TN 37068
www.ninnypublishing.com

To purchase additional copies of this book:
write to Ninny Publishing, PO Box 682882, Frankin, TN 37068,
order online at www.deadbunniesbook.com

Book Design:
Scott Lee Designs {www.scottleedesigns.com}

Web Design:
After Light Media {www.afterlightmedia.com}

Printed in the United States of America

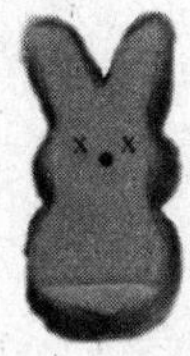

For Mom.

Because you always looked inside
me and saw a book.

Contents

Author's Note

My friend Jonathan and I once worked at a camp nestled in the Blue Ridge of North Carolina. One night a storm rolled in over the mountains that sent beautiful fireworks of lightning flashing through the sky. Sometimes the rumble hit immediately. Sometimes Jonathan and I counted to twelve before we heard the thunder boom. The storm was a magnificent display of power and art and electricity. God was showing off.

Jonathan and I spent the night running through the streets of the camp, watching the sky, and waiting for the flash and roll of a lightening bolt. When the sky lit up, Jonathan and I would shout, "Do it again! Do it again!" demanding an encore from the heavens. Within seconds, the storm would do it again. And we would enjoy another movie that God had projected on the clouds.

In my short life there have been a few moments where I thought I heard the rumble of God's voice. There have been a few instances where I was convinced I felt a flash of his presence. And I have spent every day since asking him to do it again.

I'm convinced that he does. But sometimes I have to look for it.

When I speak for worship events, someone will inevitably approach me after the service and say, "I loved the story you told about . . . . It reminds me of the time when I . . . ." And standing at the foot of a stage, we'll have beautiful conversations about God and our lives and the Bible. All because we have connected through a story.

Somewhere in that experience I've begun to realize that our stories are how we connect with one another. And it's through our stories that God and his word often connect with us. He connects with me through a conversation I had yesterday. And he does it again through something funny that happened today. And he will do yet again tomorrow if I pay attention to what's going on around me.

So I've written a little book called *Dead Bunnies*. It's a little bit silly. It's a little bit serious. It's all about the time when. *Dead Bunnies* is my personal record of the ways God has connected with me through my stories and through his scripture. These are the moments and metaphors of God in my life. They make me laugh. They make me think. Sometimes they make me wonder. I hope they'll do the same for you. But more than that, I hope these words will help you find the story of God in your own life.

"The most wasted of all days
is one without laughter."

e.e. cummings

"Laughter is carbonated holiness."

Anne Lamott

A Word of Instruction

You are about to read a book. Congratulations. I'm sure it's not your first. And I hope you're not reading because you have to or because it's very late at night and you can't fall asleep. Because some of the ideas in these pages keep me up at night. They excite me. They energize me. They challenge and sometimes terrorize me. So I'm glad we're about to talk about them. I have a few stories I'd like to tell you. And I hope you'll return the favor.

Lots of people don't understand that books aren't just words and paragraphs and paper. They're conversations.

I like conversations. I find myself talking a lot. My days are filled with words. Talking is even what I do for a living. And sometimes for recreation. But there are times when I get tired of talking. Sometimes I just want to listen. And escape. And learn. And laugh. So I pick up a book and let the words wash over me.

But I forget that the good books don't let me simply turn their pages and read their words and escape into the void. The good books don't let me close their covers and walk away no different than when I opened them. The good books invite me into their adventures. The good books challenge me to think and feel along with their characters, stories, and ideas. The good books bring me into conversations that keep me awake at night. They let me listen. But they also ask me to talk.

That's great because I want to be brought into a conversation. I want to feel connected. That's why I sing along with the radio and shout at the television. I want to be involved in the experience. I want to feel like I'm part of the story.

And so I would like to invite you into a conversation with

my dead bunnies. Get comfortable. Fix a drink. Underline. Make notes. Write down your thoughts and ideas. We have lots to talk about.

As you turn the next few pages, you're going to find a series of small pictures littering the margins of your book. These pictures will be the body language and subtle pauses that will help you know when it's your turn to talk. When you see …

Ask yourself, "How do I connect with this idea? What story do I have to tell?" I've given you a story to spark your imagination or introduce a thought, but where have you seen this idea played out in your life? If you were talking through this idea with a friend, what story would you have to tell?

Don't let your eyes pass over this sentence without thinking about it. Let this one soak in. Have a conversation with it. Do you agree with this idea? Do you disagree? Take a minute and decide how this thought could shape (or has shaped) who you are.

How do these words make you feel? Maybe you want to write a few simple words that express what happens inside you when you read these sentences. Or maybe when you see this picture, you just need to sit for a couple of seconds, stare blankly into space, and simmer in whatever this section makes you feel.

If you'd like to just read this book and get on with your life, that's fine. You have that right. But the next 176 pages will say a lot more if you will let them be a conversation.

I'll tell you my stories if you'll tell me yours.

PANAMA
HUNTSVILLE / HVS
AL 358 1 L
01 MAY PM
USA

Postcards from Panama

I recently vacationioned with some friends. I highly recommend vacationing with friends. You're obligated to enjoy family. You choose to enjoy friends. As we were in the initial stages of planning our vacation, my comrades and I declared four rules for our upcoming adventure:

Rule 1. It had to be cheap.

Rule 2. We had to use our passports. No cheating. This had to be an actual foreign country where they eat bugs or dogs or horse dung.

Rule 3. There had to be a beach that's warm and lazy even in October. The kind of beach with water so clear you can read a newspaper on the bottom. The kind of beach that makes the sun beg to wake up at the crack of dawn and rise every morning. The kind of beach that makes you feel like you are living in a Corona commercial. You get the picture.

Rule 4. Did I mention it had to be cheap?

We landed in Panama.

You might not be able to point to Panama on a map, but you should definitely go there for vacation. Maybe you're aware there is a rather large canal in Panama. It's cool. Something about a canal that's fifty-one miles long and has revolutionized world trade really makes the idea of digging ditches for a living sound a bit more noble. Any ditch that cost $375 million can't be all bad.

So we were in Panama, and we were seeing these great sights. One day I was swimming in front of our cabana and spotted a school of starfish. Or is it a constellation of starfish? Whatever, there were a bunch of them. My friend Bethany took a picture. It looked like a postcard.

Then we went to this absolutely beautiful beach on an uninhabited island that you can only reach by a twenty-five minute water taxi. It was unbelievable. On the shore we found a coconut that had just begun to sprout. It looked like one of the potatoes on top of your fridge, only cool and islandy, not weird and gross. Like a real-life Mr. Potato Head with dreadlocks. Bethany took a photo. It could be a postcard.

As we pulled back up to the main island, there was a little local boy wearing a sun-bleached T-shirt and ratty old shorts perched on the dock with one toe in the water looking like he alone understood the secret to life. Very National Geographic. Bethany took a picture. She'll probably sell it to a postcard company and make millions.

When the sun came up, she took a picture. When the sun went down, she took another picture. A pelican pooped on the water and she popped a picture. Welcome to the digital age.

Only, I kept thinking, *Put down the camera and buy a postcard.*

But postcards aren't the same. Sure, they give you the ideal picture, but it's the ideal picture through someone else's eyes. It's someone else's experience. Someone else's perfect day. A picture is different. A picture is your way of saying, "This is what it was like when *I* was there. This is what *I* saw. It was this cloudy and the waves were washing on the beach like this and those are the dolphins I saw *with my own eyes.*"

I am afraid that many of us spend our lives basically buying postcards about Jesus. We listen to stories of someone else's experience. We read books filled with someone else's explanations. And as a result we're buying someone else's faith. We are looking to find John Piper's or Donald Miller's or Beth Moore's or a youth minister's or a pastor's or our grandmother's relationship with God.

I am sure they've all had a beautiful experience. I am certain they all have a dynamic faith. I am confident they all must enjoy a unique relationship with the Lord. But it's *their* relationship. It's a postcard. And sadly, it's not for sale.

One of Jesus' best friends, a man named John, once wrote a beautiful letter, which he began by saying, "The one who existed from the beginning is the one we have heard and seen. We saw him with our own eyes and touched him with our own hands. He is Jesus Christ, the Word of life. This one who is life from God was shown to us, and we have seen him. And now we testify and announce to you that he is the one who is eternal life. He was with the Father, and then he was shown to us. We are telling you about what we ourselves have actually seen and heard, so that you may have fellowship with us. And our fellowship is with the Father and with his Son, Jesus Christ. We are writing these things so that our joy will be complete."[1]

Don't get me wrong, I'm happy to show you my pictures. I'm happy to tell you my stories. But they're mine. Wouldn't you rather have your own experience? Wouldn't you rather build your own story? Wouldn't you rather take a picture so you can say, "This is the Jesus *I* know. This is the faith *I* have experienced. This is what *I* have seen and this is how *I* felt and this is what I know about God."

We saw him with our own eyes and touched him with our own hands.

We are telling you about what we ourselves have actually seen and heard.

Be like Bethany. And John. Take a picture. It lasts longer.

John was so taken by the things he had seen and heard that he also wrote an entire book documenting the life and teachings of Jesus. At the end of his book, John said, "This is that disciple who saw these events and recorded them here. And we all know that his account of these things is accurate. And I suppose that if all the other things Jesus did were written down, the whole world could not contain the books."[2]

I think it's interesting that when John looked back on the years he had spent with Jesus, he was convinced that if all the things Jesus *did* were written down, the whole world could not contain the books. He did not comment on all the other sermons Jesus must have delivered or all the other profound truths Jesus must have taught the masses. John remembered the things Jesus *did*. He remembered the invalids Jesus healed. The prostitutes he forgave. The bread he blessed and the leftovers he provided. John remembered the water Jesus walked on and the tomb he walked out of. It seems John and the other disciples were paying attention to Jesus' life, to the big picture of his story, as much as to the individual red-letter things he said.

Jesus really got only one sermon in print. But when his disciples went to write everything down, the stories were what they remembered. The stories, both the parables he told and the actual life he lived, were Jesus' way of showing his followers the truth that is all around. And most of the time, showing is so much more effective than simply telling. Lectures are boring, but life is dynamic.

Through his stories and his life, Jesus taught that truth is to be watched as much as it is to be read. It is to be lived as much as it is to be understood. But Jesus' stories were not always easy to understand. Sometimes the truth, lesson, moral, or metaphor was hidden deep behind the characters, the setting, or even the scattered seed. His stories don't always provide us with easy answers. That's what makes Jesus such a wise and effective teacher. His stories make us think. And search. And dig. They force us to look and find the place where our lives and the great mystery of God intersect.

Jesus didn't just teach profound truth. He also taught us to look for lessons in the world around us.

A man had two sons …

A woman lost a quarter …

A farmer went out to scatter some seed …

A certain landowner planted a vineyard …

A man was going on a trip and called his servants together …

If a shepherd has one hundred sheep … [3]

The kingdom of heaven is like a treasure that a man discovered buried in a field. He was so excited about the find that he hid it again and sold everything he owned to get enough money to buy the field. And the treasure.

Jesus' stories were a way of saying, "Pay attention to God and the world around you." [4]

So pay attention to God and the world around you.

There's a great old movie theater in a collegiate section of Nashville that locals call the Village. People used to go to the Belcourt Theater to watch mainstream movies. Now they go to see art films. They also go to hear music. Good music.

The Belcourt opens into a side street in the Village, quietly escaping the attention of Nashville's star-gazing public. The theater is easily overlooked, but not easily forgotten. When people want to see a flashy concert, they follow ten thousand others to our state-of-the-art amphitheater or downtown arena to let the lights and smoke divert their attention from mediocre music. But when they want to hear cool music or see an artsy movie, Nashvillians go to the Belcourt. It is full of history, art, and style. Plus, the old seats are soft and cushioned, which counts for a lot.

Several months ago friends and I had tickets to see David Wilcox in concert at the Belcourt. Like the theater, David isn't flashy or exotic or even widely known. I have never heard his songs on the radio. But his music is good. He's from North Carolina and sings like the kind of guy who wears hiking boots and still loves his wife.

I bought two tickets to the concert, thinking I might end up taking a date. And since a couple of other friends were going, my two tickets would round the group out to four. If we went to dinner, no one would have to make the decision about who would be condemned to eat alone on one side of the booth. Walking around the Village would be less awkward if we could stroll up the sidewalk like Noah's ark, a convenient two by two. Standing in line for the doors to open would feel more balanced if there were an even number of us.

But that would require me to have a date.

I'm getting used to odd numbers.

So I decided to sell my ticket. The problem with selling a ticket before a show is that most people come to a concert with tickets in hand. And people who might still need a ticket are distrustful of anyone standing in front of a venue claiming he "accidentally" bought an extra ticket that he is willing to sell at "a good price."

People look at you like you're selling drugs or children. Like you actually want to take their scalps. But I wasn't selling drugs or children, and I'd accidentally left my tomahawk in the car. I didn't even want to make a profit from the ticket. I just wanted to cover my loss and get inside to see the concert with my friends.

But nobody was buying. They weren't even window shopping. I asked everybody. Literally. I asked people standing in line. I asked people as they approached the ticket window. I asked people walking down the street. I asked people as they put quarters into the parking meter. I even asked a jogger with a Mickey Mouse-shaped sweat stain growing down his back. He wasn't interested. Neither was Mickey.

Five minutes before the show was scheduled to start, I was still holding an extra ticket that I was willing to sell for five dollars less than what I paid for it. What a deal. But nobody wanted a deal. At the three-minute mark, I resolved to give away the ticket. For free. I mean, there's no point in a perfectly good ticket going to waste. But the sidewalks were empty. All of David's fans were comfortably nestled inside the Belcourt enjoying the padded seats I would have happily sold to them at a discounted price.

That's when the kid crossed the street, looking at his feet more than where he was going.

Why not? It was worth a try.

"Hey, man, I don't know if you care anything about seeing a concert, but I have an extra ticket. It's for the David Wilcox show that's about to start. You've probably never heard of him, but he's great. Really. If you don't want the ticket, I'm just going to end up throwing it away. I'll give it to you for free, but I've got to get inside. My friends are waiting. You probably won't like him, but do you want a ticket?"

The kid looked up with a shy grin. He probably thought I was a crazy street person trying to sell him drugs. In front of a folk concert. Can you imagine? But I wasn't trying to sell the kid drugs. I was just trying to unload a ticket and get inside before the show started. I should have left it on the sidewalk and been thankful for the extra elbow space.

"Do you want a ticket to see David Wilcox?" I asked.

"No thanks," he said sheepishly. "He's my dad."

His dad. The kid was right. He didn't need a ticket.

I found my seat just as David began to play. It was a fantastic show. During the time typically allotted for artists to introduce the band and promote their concert tour, new CD, and T-shirts for sale out back, David talked about his family. As it turned out, the tour was really just an excuse for him to take his wife and son on an extended camping trip. Between shows they drove back roads and camped in national parks, experiencing life and the road like an old Willie Nelson song. He said that his son, Nathan, loved being out of school and free to explore strange towns while his dad gave concerts for old people.

"But tonight," David announced, "Nathan decided to stick around for the show. I think he's sitting somewhere in the back. Stand up, Nathan!"

Apparently somewhere behind us Nathan stood. I didn't even turn around. We had already met.

I couldn't believe I tried to give the kid a ticket to his own dad's concert. I might as well have tried to sell Colonel Sanders a bucket of chicken. Nathan didn't need tickets to listen to his musician father perform. He travels with the man in an Airstream trailer and has heard more of his music live than I have through my iPod.

I'm a fan of David's music, but he and his son have an actual relationship. Why would Nathan pay to watch his dad from the back row of a theater when he rides with him daily in the front seat? Nathan listens to his father sing songs that were written for him, about him, and around him. His life is surrounded by what I paid to see. By what I paid double to see.

"Do you want a ticket to see David Wilcox?"

"No, thanks. He's my dad."

Of course he is.

When you bought this book, you paid to see God in print. When you handed over your cash, you may not have realized that was what you were doing, but it was. You bought a ticket. You paid for a glimpse of the divine. You paid to be entertained and enlightened. You opened to this page, hoping these words would somehow make God more real, more present, more understandable.

But this book won't show you anything you don't already

have access to. It will reveal no secrets or inside information. You've really just bought a ticket to your own dad's concert.

Christian scripture teaches that "from the time the world was created, people have seen the earth and sky and all that God made. They can clearly see his invisible qualities – his eternal power and divine nature. So they have no excuse whatsoever for not knowing God." [5]

You don't need this book to reveal God to you. God has already revealed himself to you. We live in a world that sings for him, about him, and around him. We are surrounded by God. The earth is the Lord's and everything in it. Even us. And if we are part of this creation that points all eyes to God, then our stories must somehow connect with his.

Because every life is a story God tells.

So why do we watch God from the back row when we can ride with him in the front seat? Why do we settle to observe when we can participate? Why do we wait for someone else to illustrate and explain the truth of God and his word when we can explore for ourselves and find where God has spoken through the humor and drama of our own experience and through the experience of those around us? We don't need a ticket. God has invited us into a relationship.

We saw him with our own eyes and touched him with our own hands.

We are telling you about what we ourselves have actually seen and heard.

To find God in our own stories, we have only to open our eyes and train them to see where he is peeking around the corners and whispering in the wind.

In his incredibly insightful book *Telling Secrets*, Frederick Buechner says,"It is important to tell at least from time to time the secret of who we truly and fully are — even if we tell it only to ourselves — because otherwise we run the risk of losing track of who we truly and fully are and little by little come to accept instead the highly edited version which we put forth in hope that the world will find it more acceptable than the real thing. ... I suspect that it is by entering that deep place inside us where our secrets are kept that we come perhaps closer than we do anywhere else to the One who, whether we realize it or not, is of all our secrets the most telling and the most precious we have to tell." [6]

So find your story. Explore it. Share it. In it you might hear the voice of God.

A friend of mine and I recently went to an art show titled "100 Artists See God." It was a fascinating exhibit from artists who used painting, sculpture, graphics, photography, and video to render their perception of God. And sometimes god.

In the description of his painting *All Around You and Inside You,* the artist James Gobel said that his religion has "not given me a practice, belief, or faith in God, but rather a setting and vocabulary of images and scenarios for God to exist in."

The idea that I have been given "a setting and vocabulary of images and scenarios for God to exist in" is making a nest in my brain. Like most people, my religion has not yet answered all of my questions about God and my world. My church tries, but inevitably it gets some things wrong and can't always meet all of my needs. In this well-meaning environment, however, my faith has given me a starting place to understand God and his word. It has given me the courage to explore the great mystery of God. It has given me a vocabulary of images and scenarios for that God to exist in.

Today has provided me with a setting for God to exist in.

My relationships have provided a context in which God reveals himself.

My memories are a vocabulary through which God speaks.

My stories are parables that reveal God.

My life is a story told by the divine. It is a setting and vocabulary of images and scenarios that God exists in.

But this vocabulary must begin with a very important word. Truth.

Truth [trü-th] n: the state of being the case: fact: the body of real things, events, and facts: a transcendent fundamental or spiritual reality.

It is important that as we explore how God reveals himself through the metaphor of our lives that we never begin with our story and then look for the truth hidden within. Our stories aren't a solid starting place. They're too subjective. Too unstable. Too open to interpretations that might or might not be true. When we start with our stories, we don't find the facts and fundamental spiritual reality we're looking for. When we start with our stories, we find opinion and confusing contradictions.

Instead of using our stories as a starting place for God to reveal himself, we should begin our exploration with truth and then find where that truth is demonstrated in our story. We should look to see where our lives intersect the story that God is already telling through human history and his word.

Long ago God spoke many times and in many ways to our ancestors through the prophets. But now in these final days, he has spoken to us through his Son. [7]

So the word became human and lived here on earth among us. He was full of unfailing love and faithfulness.[6]

Jesus is the Great and Mighty Oz stepping out from behind the emerald curtain.

As a result, we don't have to rely on the earth and sky to observe God's invisible qualities. It is through Jesus that God has revealed himself. In Jesus, God made himself known. And understood. And personal. And present. We are not limited to our own experience and understanding to unravel the truth.

The word (the wisdom of God) became human and lived here on earth among us. Jesus. He was full of grace and truth. This is why Christians are set on the importance of understanding and having a relationship with Jesus. To have a relationship with Jesus is to have a firsthand experience with God. And as we explore God and his truth through this relationship, we begin to see that his story really is our story.

And if we pay attention, we understand that our lives are also a story that God tells.

As you read this book, I hope that we will connect through our stories. I hope that you'll find places where our experiences, thoughts, feelings, and ideas intersect. But more than that, I hope you will recognize the moments where God has spoken through the story of your life. I hope you will learn to look for places where your story connects with the great truth and mystery of God. I hope you will realize that your stories are also metaphors through which God can speak, teach, and heal. I hope that you'll have conversations with trusted people in your life and find a place to share the secret of who you truly and fully are and what you are coming to believe about God and your world. I pray that in reflecting on our stories, you will come closer to the One who, of all our stories, is the most precious we have to tell.

Toxicodendron Radicans

Vegetarians are probably the only people on the planet who aren't at risk of being on one of those *When Animals Attack* shows. No matter how much we pretend to love animals, animals hate us. Oh sure, Champ will fetch your little stick and Fluffy will crawl into your lap and purr while you're scratching behind her ears. But they're just biding their time. When you're not home, Champ and Fluffy are curled up on the couch watching the Food Network, and it's making them very angry.

Don't get me wrong. I love animals. I do. I just love them most with barbecue sauce. Once, while shooting a video in Hawaii, I almost stepped on a wild seal. I don't love wild seals. Not even with barbeque sauce.

You'd think that stepping on a wild seal would be a difficult thing to do. But it's not as hard as you'd expect.

My friends Scott, Jeff, and I were hiking across a deserted beach on the island of Kauai when we came across a stretch of big, black shiny boulders. Imagine our surprise when, as we climbed across the rocks, we discovered that one of them wasn't a big, black shiny boulder. One of them was a living wad of fat with flippers and fangs that nature had disguised to look like a big, black shiny boulder. I almost climbed over a seal. And seals don't like to play king of the mountain. At least not when they are the mountain. Trust me.

Jesus said that if we don't praise his name, even the rocks will cry out, and apparently this rock got the memo. And took singing lessons from an orc.

I put one foot in his personal space, and the seal reared up like Flipper's demonic second cousin and growled like a bear with a rottweiler stuck in his throat. It looked as if God breathed life into a quivering heap of black Jell-O, gave it whiskers and teeth, and set it loose to run screaming onto the beach. That may not sound all that threatening to you. After all, the sound of a seal barking isn't dramatically different from the noises your brother, boyfriend, or best friend makes after eating Taco Bell. But when that sound is coming out of a wild animal that wants to eat you, it's a little unnerving.

They say that most wild animals are more afraid of us than we are of them, but "they" have obviously never been face to face with a barking lump of angry black Jell-O. The seal was too busy trying to figure out if we'd taste better with mustard or mayo to be afraid of us. I understand Darwin's survival of the fittest. And I may not be the fittest animal on the planet, but I *am* clever and I *will not* be eaten by anything that looks like the Little Mermaid's fat Uncle Ed from the Bronx.

It was awful. And the breath! It's no wonder most carnivores travel solo. Uncle Ed desperately needed an Altoid or some Listerine or a big swallow of Fabreze. When he grinned and showed us his teeth, it seemed only polite to tell him that he had something stuck between his tusks. On the left side.

"I think it might be a little piece of tourist," Scott offered. "Here, let me get that for you."

But seals aren't overly concerned with dental hygiene. Or making friends. So we moved on. And by "moved on" I mean "ran away."

After we shot our footage and were making our way back down the beach, Scott and I decided to make some mischief. Jeff had stayed behind to gather the equipment and shoot some stock images of waves and sand and safety. Scott and I climbed up a small embankment and hid behind some trees within both sight and throwing distance of the seal. Our ingenious plan was to wait until Jeff circled around the pile of boulders and then somehow anger the seal so that it would rise up and attempt to eat our friend.

Scott picked up a pine cone and prepared to throw it. I was appalled. Throwing a pine cone at a living creature? Unbelievable! "Scott, you can't throw a pine cone at that seal," I said, amazed at his irresponsibility. "It's too light. You'll never hit it. Here, use this rock!"

Any job worth doing is worth doing right.

I suppose throwing a rock at a seal probably isn't on the ASPCA's top ten list of ways to make friends with wildlife. But throwing a rock at a seal is fundamentally no different than David throwing a rock at Goliath. It's really no different than hurling spit wads at a teacher or throwing dodgeballs at that little group of girls who always huddle in a corner during a game of dodgeball. The only difference between a seal and that huddle of girls is that when you hit a wild seal in the face with a rock, it rears up and shows its teeth and flaps its fins and makes a sound like an angry fire truck. When you hit a girl in the face with a dodgeball, she rears up and shows her teeth and flaps her fins and makes a sound like an angry fire truck.

I guess maybe it's really not all that different.

So just as Jeff passed by, Scott threw a rock that bounced off the seal's blubbery side. As predicted, the animal shot up like a big, shiny, web-toed, one-footed girl playing dodgeball and hurled his animal threats. I don't speak fluent seal, but I know enough to know that what the seal barked could be loosely translated into something like, "You look yummy."

And my friend was left standing in the seal's hungry path like a Jeff McNugget, convinced he did not want his last words to be, "Please help. I'm being eaten by a seal." But Jeff was a trooper. He stood his ground, and eventually the seal backed down and scampered off into the ocean.

I honestly don't know what wildlife has to get so upset about. Every time you throw a rock at it, it gets all jumpy. Every time you shoot at it, it flies away. Every time you aim your car at it, it runs into the bushes. Why can't animals just be a little more social?

It's probably because they've learned their lesson. Wildlife hides from people because people throw rocks at wildlife.

And people hide from one another because we do the same thing.

Jesus went to the Mount of Olives. At dawn he appeared again in the temple courts, where all the people gathered around him, and he sat down to teach them. The teachers of the law and the Pharisees brought in a woman caught in adultery. They made her stand before the group and said to Jesus, "Teacher, this woman was caught in the act of adultery. In the Law Moses commanded us to stone such women. Now what do you say?" They were using this question as a trap, in order to have a basis for accusing him.

But Jesus bent down and started to write on the ground with his finger. When they kept on questioning him, he straightened up and said to them, "If any one of you is without sin, let him be the first to throw a stone at her." Again he stooped down and wrote on the ground.

At this, those who heard began to go away one at a time, the older ones first, until only Jesus was left, with the woman still standing there. Jesus straightened up and asked her, "Woman, where are they? Has no one condemned you?"

"No one, sir," she said.

"Then neither do I condemn you," Jesus declared. "Go now and leave your life of sin." [1]

I often tell people there's no reason for them to hide or be afraid. God is compassionate and not easily angered. He keeps no record of wrong. He's not in the stone throwing business.

Unfortunately, the rest of us are.

It's no wonder we live camouflaged lives among the rocks, trying desperately to blend in and escape notice. It's no wonder we hide from one another. I don't need stone throwing. My mistakes hurt enough without anyone making me feel worse with their moral superiority. I don't need judgment. What I need is acceptance and understanding. What I need is a safe place to hide.

I can think of no safer place than Jesus' phrase "then neither do I condemn you."

There are certain of life's smaller pleasures that you have to have testosterone to understand. The freedom of peeing outside. The joy of driving through a deep puddle. The exhilaration of shooting bottle rockets at your neighbor's house and/or pets. When you're a man, these are the things that make life worth living.

For some reason, the more dangerous or destructive the adventure, the more we like it. As boys, our lives are filled with an unquenchable desire to step on, hit, swat, or shoot at anything that moves and isn't directly related to us. Most of the time we're even willing to ignore the "isn't directly related to us" clause. We are, by nature, aggressive.

Sometimes, when we're walking through the woods wearing camo, splashed with deer urine, and shooting at various animals named Bambi, we label our aggression "sport." Sometimes, when we're walking through the woods painted army green and shooting small balls of paint at our friends, we call our aggression "game." Other times, when we're not in the woods at all, and we're simply thumping, pushing, shoving, and/or hitting another human, it's just plain fun.

As I said, there are certain things you have to have testosterone to understand.

I think paintball must be one of those things. Paintball is a marvelous game where opposing teams attack each other with guns that use highly compressed air to shoot small wads of paint. Guys like to play paintball because it's primal. Shooting is a rush. Being shot at is a rush. It reminds us of days when we were kids and ran around in the woods with swords that were really just long sticks and fought trees and threw rocks and shot bottle rockets at each other.

Granted, some girls also like to run around in the woods shooting paint at people. These girls are to be feared. Females who take pleasure in shooting at guys are dangerous. Especially if they giggle. Many girls, however, don't understand the goodness of paintball. They think, *Why would you dress up in smelly old camos you got at Goodwill and smear black junk all over your face and run around and get sweaty and let people shoot at you?*

Boys know this is a ridiculous question. We do it because we get to dress up in smelly old camos we got at Goodwill and smear black junk all over our faces and run around and get sweaty and let people shoot at us. It's like playing a video game, except that when you get shot, you actually get shot. With paint. Yellow. Green. Blue. Paint.

If you can imagine what would happen if the Teletubbies crossed Sesame Street and started a gang war, it would be like that. Colorful carnage. Ernie meets vice city. Elmo on the west side. You walk into the woods looking like Rambo. You walk out of the woods looking like a Skittles commercial.

My friend Jonathan was getting married recently and wanted to play paintball for his bachelor party. Paintball is a fitting bachelor party activity. I don't know if you've ever attended a bachelor party, but you should. Basically, it's a guy's way of saying goodbye to one life and hello to another. He's leaving a world of midnight pizza runs, farting contests, and video games (in other words, everything good and holy), and entering a world of minivans, scented candles, Tupperware parties, and some chick asking him if these pants make her look fat. That's why paintball makes a great bachelor party. We're your friends. We'll shoot you before we let that happen.

About ten of us showed up for Jonathan's bachelor party shoot out. We suited up in camo, painted our faces, grabbed our guns, goggles, and air cylinders, and prepared for the ensuing annihilation. The best man brought ammo. Yellow.

In case you've never seen a paintball, it's a little marble-sized sphere of paint covered in … something. They say the outer coating is thin plastic or gelatin that bursts on contact. Gelatin is the stuff they make Jell-O out of. When you get hit with a paintball, however, it doesn't feel like getting hit with Jell-O. Jell-O is wiggly, giggly fun. When you get hit in the neck with one of these things it doesn't feel like wiggly, giggly, fun. It feels like being bitten by a polar bear. It hurts.

And that's just what happened during our first game. I got shot in the neck.

I couldn't believe my luck. There I sat, hiding behind a tree, practically invisible, when a guy from the other team crossed right in front of me and stopped. Still. Breathless. Clueless of the paint-covered pain in his immediate future. I had the perfect shot. This guy was about to be wasted. Torn up. Covered in yellow. I was going to make him look like he had been sitting under Big Bird at a chili eating contest.

But as soon as I stuck my head out to take the shot, it happened. Someone had been watching. Patiently. Waiting for his moment. And I gave it to him. And he gave it to me. In the neck. And it hurt.

All I could feel was immediate throbbing pain as a freakish welt rose and a beautiful purple bruise seeped to the surface. This was extra special because the next day I was going to be standing on a stage, looking great in a tux next to my buddy, the groom, with a big paintball hickey on my neck. Classy.

And people would say, "Nice hickey!"

And I would say, "It's not what you think. I got it at the bachelor party last night."

And they would say, "Yeah, I bet you did."

Needless to say, I may have been shot, but I did not just stand there wallowing in pain and paint. As soon as my brain registered that I was hit and therefore in trouble, I tore through the woods looking for a new place to hide.

See, we had a two-shot dead rule. This means you had to be shot twice before you die. The beauty of the two-shot dead rule is that once you've been hit, you don't have the luxury of throwing up your hands and surrendering. You don't have the safety of knowing that the rules of sportsmanship dictate that your buddy won't shoot you again. When playing two-shot dead, the first shot is just a wake-up call. If your friend was able to shoot you once, that means he is probably able to do it again. And if you are stupid enough to sit still, he will.

So after being shot the first time, I ran through the woods looking for bushes that would provide cover. Luckily, I found the ideal spot — a big tree surrounded by a leafy bush that provided the perfect hole in which to lick my wounds. As I sat there in this tangle of green, I remembered that right before I left for the party, my good friend Mel had said, "Be careful playing paintball. You might get poison ivy." She didn't say, "Be careful that you don't get your eye shot out" or, "Be careful that you don't die." No, she said, "Be careful of poison ivy."

Be careful of plants. In the woods. Thanks.

And I had laughed. I laughed because she clearly didn't catch the vision of paintball. When you're running through the woods trying to save your own Private Ryan, being careful is not on the menu. When that first shot whizzes past your face at fifty feet per second and explodes on a tree next to you, you do not stop to think, *Look at that vine! It has the three leaf cluster characteristic of toxicodendron radicans, more commonly known as poison ivy. If I touch it, it will cause an uncomfortable and unsightly rash. I should steer clear!*

No, the only thing you think in this situation is, *I just got shot at! This is so cool.*

And that's exactly what I thought as I sat there in what I believed was a bush but was actually a bush covered in poison ivy. It wasn't until later, when my skin was itchy and oozing and angry that I realized diving into a thicket of unknown brush may not have been a super smart thing to do. When my arms and legs itched so badly that I began to consider amputation as a valid form of relief, it occurred to me that just standing still and letting the polar bear give me another hickey might not have been such a bad idea after all.

I understand that making people itch is just the poison ivy's defense mechanism. It is only doing its job. You get too close, and the plant feels like it has to defend itself. But the poison ivy did not need to defend itself against me. It's not as if I had threatened its young. I didn't attack it or try to eat it. I only brushed up against it. I just wanted a place to hide. Apparently, poison ivy has some serious issues with personal space.

I respect not wanting to be touched. I understand needing space. But most creatures at least give you some sort of warning. Animals very clearly let you know that they don't want to be touched. Try to hug a pit bull and he'll quickly let you know that he kissed dating goodbye. So if you're a plant and you want some space, give us some warning please. Cover yourself with big, angry thorns that scream, "Get off me or I'll cut you!" Don't just hang out looking all green and leafy and innocent as you plot to make my life miserable. That's not fair. Especially when I just want a place to hide.

I know plenty of people who live their entire lives on the defensive. They feel like the whole world is taking shots at them, plotting to make their life miserable. They live so carefully, so guarded, so convinced that everyone is watching, waiting for them to fall and make fools of themselves.

And maybe we are.

But it makes my heart sad to see so many good people wandering through life, looking for a safe place to hide. Looking for a relationship or job or degree program or movie or portable gaming device or iPod that will insulate them from the world. The shots have been so real and so painful that they just want to be sure that they don't get hit again.

Good luck with that.

Unfortunately, many of the places people hide don't end up being as safe as they had hoped. The relationship. The sex.

The job. The philosophy. The distractions. Sometimes these are just empty. But sometimes they leave us even more damaged than we were when we started.

Sometimes we wish we had been more careful. But sometimes the pain is so intense that we're tempted to just give up and let the polar bear have his way.

For those of us who have found a relationship with God, that's part of the appeal. The safe place. In a chaotic, busy, stressful, and sometimes hurtful world, we've found a place of genuine peace and safety. It's not that we don't still get shot at. It's not that the shots don't still connect and hurt sometimes. It's just that our wounds aren't the marks that define us. We don't live according the bad that people have done to us. We live according to the good that God has done for us.

We've been given a place to hide.

Would you like to hear a revelation that has changed my life? Can I share something with you that has made my days a lot less stressful? I've recently begun to realize that ...

- Everyone is not watching me all the time, so I can quit acting and performing like everyone is watching me.
- Everyone is not thinking about me all the time, so I don't have to be paranoid about what other people think of me.
- Everyone does not do things knowing how certain actions will affect me, so I can quit getting my feelings hurt about everything.
- I am not the center of the universe's attention. So when my mind is clear enough to realize this, I can rest. I can relax. I can let my guard down. Nobody is watching. Nobody is waiting to take a second shot.

In the Bible, a man named Isaiah once said, "Look up into the heavens. Who created all the stars? He brings them out one after another, calling each by its name. And he counts them to see that none are lost or have strayed away. So how can you say the Lord does not see your troubles? How can you say God refuses to hear your case?"[2]

Did you know that if you hold your thumb up to the night sky, it blocks approximately one hundred thousand galaxies, most of which you can't even see? Each of these galaxies has fifty to one hundred billion stars. Do the math. That means your thumb covers over five zillion stars. I don't even know where the commas go in five zillion. That's just what my puny little thumb blocks out. And I can't even see the whole sky. Most of it is busy covering the other side of our planet.

Look up into the heavens. Who created all those stars? He brings them out one after another, calling each by its name. And he counts them to see that none are lost or have strayed away.

He calls them each by name. He counts them and knows if even one is missing. Apparently God knows where all the commas go.

What surprises me is not that God took the time to make the stars, but that he takes the time to *know* them. He doesn't just know their names, he *calls* their names. He keeps up with them. It is his power that keeps them in line. He is actively involved with each one enough to count them and see that none are lost or have strayed away.

If that's true, how can I say the Lord does not see *my* troubles? How can I say God refuses to hear *my* case? What makes me think that God doesn't notice and miss me when I've wandered off?

He calls each by name. I may not be the center of the world's attention, but I am in the center of God's attention.

I said earlier that nobody is constantly watching you. That may not be entirely true. Apparently God is watching. But despite what may have been yelled at you from some well-meaning preacher, I don't think God is watching because he wants to catch you at something. I don't think he's watching because he doesn't trust you. I don't think he's watching like a couch-junkie getting his reality TV fix. He's not a voyeur. He's not making a list and checking it twice, trying to find out who's naughty and nice. In fact, I'm not even sure that I'm completely comfortable saying, "God is watching us." That sounds a little creepy. (Santa Claus seeing me when I'm sleeping always felt a little creepy too.)

Watching is such an intense word. Maybe instead of "God is watching," it's more accurate to say that God is paying attention. And he's not just paying attention to the universe. He's paying attention to me. As I run through the woods of life, he's ready to give me a safe place to hide.

How can you say the Lord does not see your troubles? How can you say God refuses to hear your case? Have you never heard or understood? Don't you know that the Lord is the everlasting God, the Creator of all the earth? He never grows faint or weary. No one can measure the depths of his understanding. He gives power to those who are tired and worn out; he offers strength to the weak. Even youths will become exhausted, and young men will give up. But those who wait on the Lord will find new strength. They will fly high on wings like eagles. They will run and not grow weary. They will walk and not grow faint. [3]

God is paying attention, and he sees that people become exhausted. Worn out. Tired. Exhausted in a way that has nothing to do with sleep. You're tired of looking in the mirror and hating what you see. You're tired of working so hard for people to like you. You're tired of working so hard to understand. And be loved by God.

You're tired. But he's paying attention.

He is paying attention, and he understands that even the young will give up. They stumble and fall. You signed the card, but true love didn't wait. You get drunk on Friday night, sleep in on Saturday, and go to church on Sunday morning trying to convince yourself of ... something. Your computer screen has seen more naked people than a YMCA locker room. You've stumbled and fallen. But he is paying attention.

Those who wait on the Lord will find new strength. They will fly high on wings like eagles. They will run and not grow weary. They will walk and not grow faint.

You're tired, but the race isn't over. You've been shot, but you're not out of the game. You just need to find a better place to hide.

So wait. On the Lord. Wait. Flying, running, and even walking may not happen immediately. Finding new strength will probably require that you hide and rest for a few minutes. So take a few minutes.

Nobody is watching.

MINT.

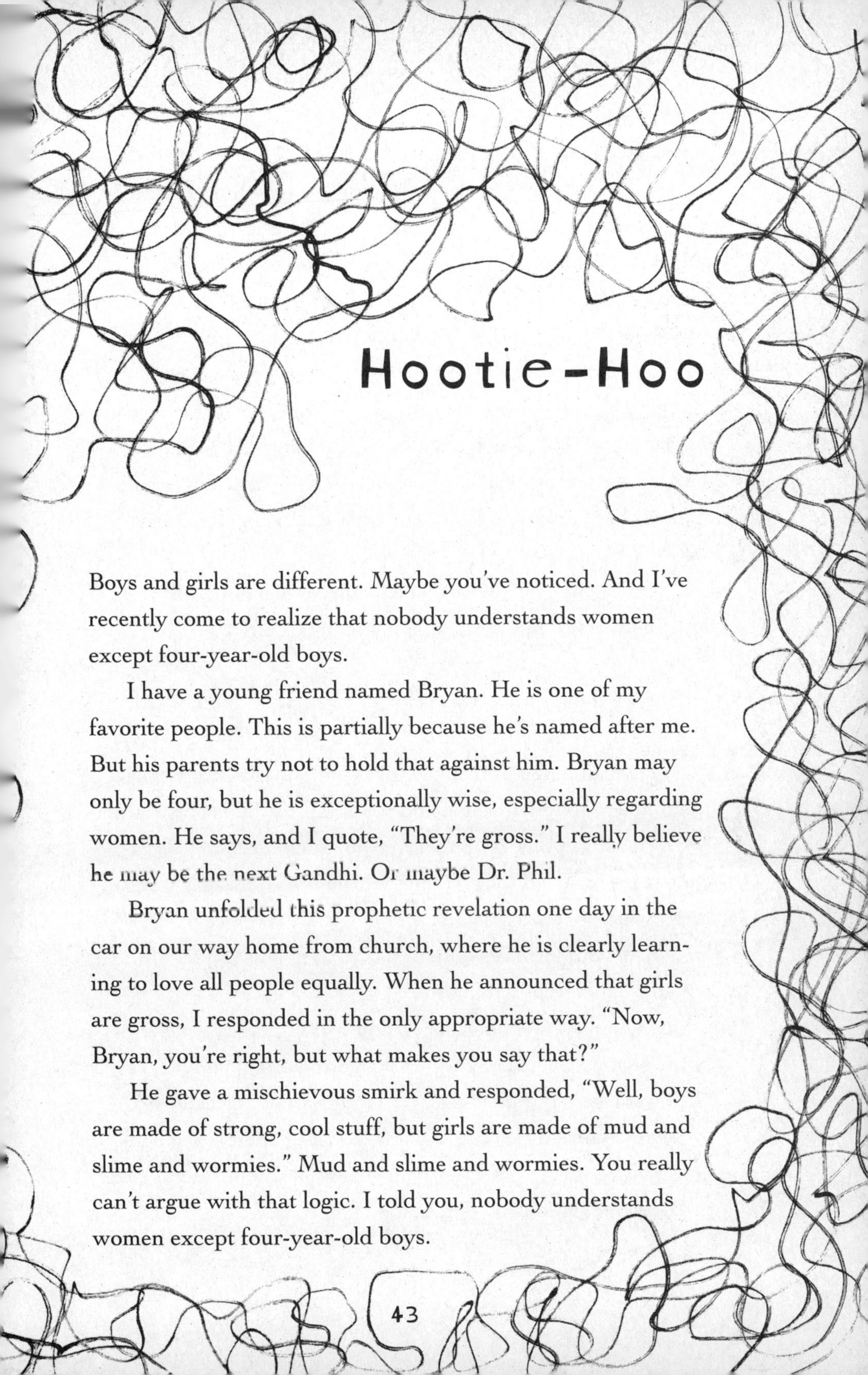

Hootie-Hoo

Boys and girls are different. Maybe you've noticed. And I've recently come to realize that nobody understands women except four-year-old boys.

I have a young friend named Bryan. He is one of my favorite people. This is partially because he's named after me. But his parents try not to hold that against him. Bryan may only be four, but he is exceptionally wise, especially regarding women. He says, and I quote, "They're gross." I really believe he may be the next Gandhi. Or maybe Dr. Phil.

Bryan unfolded this prophetic revelation one day in the car on our way home from church, where he is clearly learning to love all people equally. When he announced that girls are gross, I responded in the only appropriate way. "Now, Bryan, you're right, but what makes you say that?"

He gave a mischievous smirk and responded, "Well, boys are made of strong, cool stuff, but girls are made of mud and slime and wormies." Mud and slime and wormies. You really can't argue with that logic. I told you, nobody understands women except four-year-old boys.

About the time he made this observation, we passed a construction site where they were building a new Super Target, or Mega Wal-Mart, or some other retail shopping monster. It had been raining in southern Florida, so the site was muddy and sloppy and gross. Bryan looked out his window and saw the construction workers trudging through the mud, slime, and wormies and asked, "Big Bryan, what are those men doing?" (Since I'm considerably bigger than he is, Bryan calls me Big Bryan. This helps with the confusion when Bryan's mom, Lisa, needs to scold someone for throwing Cheerios or making loud noises. It keeps the little guy from needlessly taking blame.)

Seeing this as a wonderful teaching opportunity, I turned and answered, "Apparently they're making girls."

Bryan thought that was very funny. Bryan's mother did not.

I have an older sister named Kathy. She is a girl, but she's not made of mud and slime and wormies. Kathy is one of the exceptions. I got lucky. She never punched me, shoved me, shot at me, or tried to catch my hair on fire. Actually, I was doubly lucky because Kathy was generally too nice to tell on me when I did most of those things to her. This is a fact for which I am eternally thankful.

As a family, my mom, sister, and I used to take road trips in the summer. Usually we vacationed to very exotic places like Arkansas. For one week we would drive to Arkansas to see my aunt, uncle, and cousins. As an elementary school kid, it was a long eight-hour drive from Nashville, Tennessee, to Batesville, Arkansas. Time stood still somewhere around

Memphis. And this was back in a day before mini-vans and DVD players and Game Boys. This was back when the speed limit was 55 mph, and the only thing you could do to entertain yourself on a long trip was play car games.

Car games. I Spy, Twenty Questions, The Alphabet Game, and License Plate Bingo. My personal favorite was a game that I invented. It was called "Wipe a Booger on Your Sister." For some reason nobody else ever wanted to play.

On one particularly memorable trip, my sister and I attempted to stave off boredom by having a burping contest. A few paragraphs ago you may have been offended when I obviously approved of Bryan's saying that girls are made of mud and slime and wormies. You may feel that women are sweet, delicate flowers who are to be respected and treasured. I don't disagree. My sister is a beautiful woman.

But all qualified burping connoisseurs agree that you haven't heard a good burp until you've heard a good girl burp. And when my sister chugged a warm coke and opened her mouth, the sound that exploded from her face was nothing short of artistic. Beast came out of the beauty. It was disgusting, gross, and awesome. But I knew I could do better.

So I swallowed my Dr. Pepper in one gulp and began to feel the power develop deep within me. And when I opened my mouth to release the force and fury, it was frightening. Wet and frightening. Kathy and I laughed so hard, I may have peed in my pants. But my mother was not amused. She had lost her sense of humor somewhere between Little Rock and me practically throwing up in her hair. So she turned, looked me in the eye, and said, "Bryan Neil Currie, just stop that."

"But I can't help it," I lied.

"Yes, you can help it," she countered. "The next time you do that, just say, 'Pardon me, please' and let that be the end of it."

Now, when you've spent the better part of your life getting in trouble for various lapses in judgment, you tend to learn when people mean business and when they don't. My mother meant business. Unfortunately, just because you hit a home run doesn't mean there's not another batter on deck. I may have let the Alien out, but Predator was still on his way.

I tried to be good. I really did. I tried. But the pressure was building. And I forgot. I opened my mouth to sing along with the radio. It was an innocent enough thing to do. I wanted to sing. To make a joyful noise. Unfortunately, joyful was not on the menu that day. Even though the radio told me that the Devil went down to Georgia, that day he lived in my gut. And when I opened my mouth to sing, he escaped. He escaped with a rumbling that would have exorcised Emily Rose. I was a man possessed. It was awful. And loud.

My mother had had enough. From the front seat she turned around and gave me that look that lets you know your life is about to end. I think flames may have shot out of her face. I wanted to encourage her to keep her eyes on the road, but perhaps it wasn't the best time. She glared at me and said, "Bryan ... what ... did ... I ... tell ... you ... to ... say?"

I obediently responded, "Pardonmeplease ... and let that be the end of it."

And as the car skidded to an abrupt halt on the side of the road, I knew that wasn't going to be the end of it. But it might be the end of me.

She wanted me to "just stop." The problem was, she didn't understand that I couldn't just stop. There was a swelling inside me that begged to come out. I couldn't just stop any more than rain can just stop falling or geese can just stop flying south or Michael Jackson can just stop being a freak.

Just stop? Please.

When I go to church it seems that's the same message I hear. Just stop. You're having sex before you're married? Just stop. You're smoking pot? Just stop. You think about things that would make your mother cry and your grandmother ask awkward questions? Just stop. You're partying with friends? Just stop. You're using your computer to look at naked people? Just stop.

You're human and can't seem to keep that from being a problem? Well, just stop it.

I wish it were that easy. The problem is, there's this rumbling inside me that begs to get out. In the Bible, Paul calls it my "sinful nature." My spirit wants to do what is right, but my mind and body do not always obey. Just stop? Please.

One of the problems with the "just stop" philosophy is that I have gotten trapped into thinking that God simply wants to transform my actions. He only wants me to behave better. The trouble with this idea is that I begin to believe that if I behave better, then I will earn God's love. If I act right, then somehow God will be obligated to be impressed by me.

But I don't know why God would be impressed by what I do, considering he also knows what I think and feel. He is completely aware of this rumbling in my soul. If he were ever impressed by what's on my outside, then what goes on inside would definitely change that impression.

But the beautiful thing is that when the rumbling does make its way to the surface, the Bible basically teaches that when I say, "Pardon me, please," he lets that be the end of it. Of course, forgiveness assumes that I will try to do better next time. But even if I don't, the trip isn't over. The car doesn't come to a screeching halt. He doesn't make me walk home. I try again. And again.

In my darker moments I find that idea to be completely unbelievable. I cannot comprehend that anything so generous could really be that easy. But it's in those darker moments that I most need it to be true.

Pardon me, please. And let that be the end of it.

In the old days, monks would sit in monasteries and chant a similar request. For hours upon hours they would repeat, "God, have mercy on me, a sinner." I'm pretty sure once would have been enough. But maybe they weren't repeating the prayer for God. Maybe they were repeating it for themselves.

God, have mercy on me, a sinner.

Pardon me please. And let that be the end of it.

Just because he does, doesn't mean that I do. Maybe I should.

Why do men make idiots of themselves in the presence of women? Is it hormonal or do we just not know better? Maybe we have fooled ourselves into thinking that any attention is good attention.

It's not.

This craving for acknowledgement from the fairer sex is what prompted my buddies and me to climb into my Jeep and go hootie-hooing one warm spring night. Although you may not be familiar with the details of this activity, you should know that every dude has hootie-hoo'd. If not with their mouths, at least in their minds.

Hootie-hooing is what happens when a group of guys gets together and drives aimlessly until they see a girl they feel is worth making a fool of themselves for. When they find such a creature, they roll down the window, stick out their heads, and yell, "Hootie-Hoo!" (While other guys have developed variations on this theme, including such phrases as "hey baby!" and "look over here," we've found "hootie-hoo" to be by far the most effective and least offensive option.) Once the guy has given the girl a hootie-hoo, it is then the girl's turn to return a dirty look. Or her favorite finger. Or both.

For some reason, girls don't always understand that the hootie-hoo is a compliment. If you go to a concert and the band plays a song you like, you clap or yell or throw something. If you go to a nice restaurant and have a good meal, you send your compliments the chef. If you see a beautiful painting in a museum, you nod your head knowingly and say, "Hmmm." These are our ways of saying, "Thanks. You did a great job. Keep up the good work." Girls don't typically understand that the hootie-hoo is not actually about them. The hootie-hoo is really just a guy's way of telling God, "Good job."

So one night my friend Jordan and his brother, Jeremy, and I took the top off my Jeep and went hootie-hooing in

Panama City Beach, Florida. It was spring break and we had been hired to lead worship for a Christian camp on the beach. As single guys, a bit of hootie-hooing seemed like a wonderful way to spend the evening. To top off our worship experience, we were simply going to spend some time admiring God's creation. Specifically, his blonde creation.

While we were out, Jeremy asked if we could stop at the big pier that juts out into the Gulf from the middle of town. He wanted to stop because the week before he had helped catch a 780-pound shark off of this very pier. A 780-pound shark. That's a shark the size of a minivan. And like a minvan, it was probably full of children. Do you realize what kind of bait you would have to use to catch a 780-pound shark? To catch an average fish in an average lake in Nashville, you would use a minnow no bigger than your thumb. To catch a 780-pound shark, you would have to use a third grader. And that's not a very responsible use of a third grader.

We stopped at the pier because we wanted to see what other man-eating creatures were being caught that night. Unfortunately, there were none. But as we climbed back into the Jeep, two college guys walked up and asked for a ride to their hotel, which was apparently a couple of miles down the beach.

It has to be understood that it was 11:30 at night, in Panama City Beach, during spring break. These guys were so drunk they were flammable. Please don't misunderstand. I don't mind giving Jack Daniels and his friend a ride. I would rather they be in my car than in their own vehicle turning the roads into a real-life Mario Cart. But I have to admit, there's a short list of rules that I maintain in regard to what I allow in my vehicle:

Rule 1: I don't allow smoking in my car.
Rule 2: I don't allow any music by anyone named Justin, Brittany, or Jessica to be played in my car.
Rule 3: I don't allow any angry, sharp-toothed animals in my car.
Rule 4: I will not have people vomiting in my car.

To be honest, these guys didn't have cigarettes in their mouths, they weren't humming "Oops I Did It Again," and they didn't appear to be in possession of angry wolverines. But you could tell from the white of their faces and the water in their eyes that they were about to violate Rule 4.

Rule 4 clearly states that once dinner has gone in the top, it doesn't need to come back out again until the bottom. It's the circle of life. All drains lead to the ocean. Garbage in, garbage out. That's the way the cycle goes. And both of these guys were about to reverse the cycle.

So I was completely honest with them. I said, "Guys, I'd love to give you a ride, but I can't have you blowing groceries in my car."

The less pickled of the two managed to say, "No, man, we're fine. Really." Just as he swallowed something large and unpleasant.

And I thought, *Yeah, you look like you're fine. What you really are is full of it, and it looks like it isn't going to be long before you empty some of it back out. But not in my car.*

You hate to do it, but sometimes you have to just say no, and I did. Nancy Reagan would have been proud. It was the right decision. As we swung a U-turn and pulled back by the spot where the guys were standing, both of them were bent over double with their heads in the bushes. From what I could hear, they were either becoming violently ill or singing the shrubs a song. If they were serenading the bushes, they had the worst singing voices I have ever heard. If not, I made a wise decision by not letting them in my car. If I had not stood strong in my no, I would have been sitting in the front seat with a lap full of leftovers.

And that would definitely ruin a good hootie-hoo.

The college guys said they were fine. But they weren't. They were full of it. It was spring break and they had been drinking way too much. When you drink way too much, it is inevitable that some of it will come back up and out. That's the nature of the beast. When you overfill yourself with something intoxicating, you eventually have to deal with it again. Just not in my car.

That's what scares me most about myself. Not that I'll get sick in my car, but that my sin will find me out. I am afraid that it will come back up.

I am afraid that I've overfilled myself with garbage (intoxicating though it may be) that I will never be finished dealing with. Part of that fear probably comes from the shame I feel when I confess my numerous shortcomings and bad decisions to God. I am horrified and embarrassed when I realize what I'm actually capable of. But my fear goes deeper than embarrassment and guilt.

My real fear is that maybe I'm not done with my darkest deeds. I'm scared that I can't control what's going on inside me, what I've filled myself with. I'm scared that even though

I have confessed my sin, and God has been faithful and just to forgive my sin and cleanse me of every unrighteousness, the struggle isn't over. I've said, "Pardon me, please." But I am afraid that's not the end of it. I still find myself doing and thinking the things I thought Jesus was supposed to set me free from. My sins (and the temptations that cause them) still find me. And I don't understand.

I'm not fine, but I want to be. I want to be rid of the filth that I have filled myself with. I really do. But when I pray and ask God for his precious forgiveness, there is almost always a tickle in my soul that reminds me. It reminds me that even though I am fundamentally sorry for doing whatever it is that I'm asking forgiveness for, I probably still want to do it again. My regret does not negate my desire. Even though I'm sorry, I am also relatively certain that tomorrow, when the emotions of my remorse wear off, I will still want to fall into the same trap again. And again. And the cycle will continue.

And that scares me.

Because even though I know in my heart that I'm supposed to be set free from sin, in my mind I still feel like I'm full of it.

A very real part of me wants to say that all I have to do is figure out a way to empty myself of my own weakness. I just have to purge. I want to point to Bible passages that say things like, "Now is the time to get rid of anger, rage malicious behavior, slander, and dirty language. Don't lie to each other, for you have stripped off your old evil nature and all its wicked deeds. In its place you have clothed yourselves with a new nature that is continually being renewed as you learn more and more about Christ, who created this new nature within you." [4]

I want to read the part in scripture that reminds myself to "throw off [my] old evil nature and [my] former way of life, which is rotten through and through, full of lust and deception. Instead, there must be a spiritual renewal of [my] thoughts and attitudes. [I] must display a new nature because [I am] a new person, created in God's likeness — righteous, holy, and pure." [5]

I want to connect with these ideas because I know that *get rid of* and *throw off* literally mean "remove" or "get as far away from you as you can." They don't exactly mean "vomit out the poison," but close. And that feels right. That feels like what I should do. What I want to do.

I want to empty myself of my former way of life that is rotten through and through, full of lust and deception. I want to purge the garbage that sickens my soul so that I can feel better. I want to strip the old and put on the new. I want to start over. And I assume that if emptying the contents of a spoiled stomach generally makes me feel better, then throwing off the leftovers of a former life must feel just as good.

But I also know that even when I want to do right, wrong is just around the corner.

Like batteries or cigarette lighters, a duplex is a house that comes in a two-pack. I used to live in a two-pack, with my house and the house next door snuggled together like conjoined twins. In addition to sharing a wall, my house and my neighbor's house shared a sidewalk and front porch. Because each half of the duplex was a mirror image of the other, the top of our front stairs forced visitors into the decision of either turning left into my neighbor's front door or right into mine. I knew that my neighbor's name was Mike, but that was almost all I knew about him. Every now and then he and I would meet as I pulled into the driveway and he pulled out. We'd wave. Sometimes I would try to speak when we passed on the sidewalk, but Mike never had much to say.

Then one day I was standing in the kitchen eating a bowl of cereal without my pants. Or my shirt. Or any of my clothes whatsoever. It was laundry day. And sometimes a man's Lucky Charms need to be enjoyed in the freedom of an all-natural environment. I would never eat this way in public, but how a person chooses to enjoy his breakfast in the privacy of his own kitchen is his own business. Cereal requires milk, a bowl, and a spoon. It doesn't require pants. And even the milk is optional.

On this particular morning, as I was enjoying my freedom and cereal, Mike decided to peek into my kitchen window on his way home from the midnight shift. I lifted my spoon to wave hello, but Mike was visibly shaken by what he saw. He didn't wave back. I don't know what his problem was. What did he expect, that I was going to invite him in for a bagel? The situation was already awkward enough with me standing naked holding a bowl of cereal with only a window between us. Opening the door would be plain weird.

Mike and I didn't talk much after that.

Our duplex was right next to the interstate. My house and I-24 were so intimate that the D.O.T. sometimes referred to our front yard as the shoulder. Several organizations even offered to adopt the driveway as a service project and were disappointed when told that it was actually private property.

"We wondered," they said "why your mile marker has a little red flag and a handle."

Sometimes, especially during rush hour, getting the mail did present a bit of a challenge.

To escape both the constant noise of passing traffic and my peekaboo neighbor, I liked to go jogging in the afternoons. Running really is a great way to clear your mind if you don't mind the oxygen deprivation, dehydration, sweating, and misery that goes with it. One day as I was running and trying to burn the calories that I sometimes find free in a box of Oreos, I heard a strange and wonderful sound ring through the neighborhood. The bells reminded me of fairies. The song of the circus.

The ice cream truck was coming.

What a cruel trick of nature. What an ironic twist of fate to exercise while being chased by an ice cream truck. Being chased by Dobermans is excellent motivation to run faster. Being chased by an ice cream truck is not. The truck's siren song did not motivate me to run. It motivated me to squat down on the sidewalk and fill my sweating face with ice-cold goodness. And even though I resisted and continued my pace, the devil woman with her Fudgesicles and Nutty Buddies drew ever closer. Her truck was yellow. Her music merry. Her cargo delicious.

But even Satan appears as an angel of light.

It took all of my willpower to let the ice cream lady drive by without flagging her down for a creamy, chocolatey treat. That, and the knowledge that I don't carry money when I run.

I got all the way to an elementary school that was about two miles from my house. The school's parking lot served as my turn-around spot. It was nice to see children playing on the playground when I made my loop. Their youthful energy and innocence served as an inspiration not to succumb to the pounding heart attack developing in my oxygen-deprived chest.

But my distressed heart would not be my downfall on this fateful day. Neither would my heaving lungs. On this day my feet proved to be the enemy, along with one ill-placed rock.

I am not an accomplished runner. I am neither graceful nor quick. But I have been using my feet for quite some time and like to think that I have at least mastered their basic skills. The left foot steps in front of the right, which steps in front of the left, each falling into place one after the other. It's an easy rhythm. A basic technique.

Until you trip.

In the elementary school parking lot, I tripped. Over a rock. A small rock. I tripped over a rock that was so small it had only been promoted from sand the week before. Of course, it was also only a small stone that fell the mighty giant Goliath. But his stone was hurled from a sling. Mine wasn't. Mine was just sitting in the parking lot, patiently waiting for school to be let out.

When my right foot stumbled, I tried to recover with my left. But when I did, the foot landed badly. It turned, and my entire body weight was caught on the side of my foot. Not the bottom. The side. Where the foot becomes an ankle and is no longer built to be stepped on.

If you have ever sprained your ankle, you know how much it hurts. You know that you would rather have a tooth pulled by a four-year-old child with a pair of tin snips than to have it happen again. As I turned my ankle that day and heard the tendon-tearing pop that sent me spread-eagle into the elementary school parking lot, the world went dark. Pain filled my body and brain and shot out of my mouth in a language that most Christians try to avoid.

I don't make a habit of using the words that sound like bleeps when someone says them on network television, but sometimes pain overrides the censor.

When I shouted, several children on the playground turned, shocked at what they had heard. I wanted to apologize. I wanted them to understand that I didn't mean to use bad words. What I meant to say was, "Quick, call 911." But they didn't understand. They didn't feel my pain. They also didn't call 911.

So I sat in the parking lot with tears in my eyes, looking forward to hobbling two miles home with a growth the size of a baseball swelling out of my sock.

But then I heard it. Fairy bells. A circus song. The ice cream lady in her blessed yellow truck was coming to save the day. Maybe she wasn't a devil woman after all. Maybe she would stop to give me an Astro-Pop to dry my tears and a Sno-Cone to reduce the swelling. Maybe she would give me a ride home.

Or maybe she would ignore the sweaty heap of weeping flesh sprawled in the parking lot and drive on to paying customers who could happily skip and run to her with handfuls of money.

I couldn't skip. I couldn't run. I had no money. And I wasn't happy.

She didn't stop.

This time what I yelled wasn't an accident.

I thought I had at least the basics of running figured out. But then something as small as a stone came along and landed me flat on my face. It's usually when I think I have everything figured out that I let my guard down and get tripped up by the little things. And that's when I find my humility. When I am flat on my face.

But I'm not alone. Even heroes of the Bible tripped. Paul wrote, "But to keep me from getting puffed up, I was given a thorn in my flesh, a messenger from Satan to torment me and keep me from getting proud. Three different times I begged the Lord to take it away. Each time he said, 'My gracious favor is all you need. My power works best in your weakness.' So now I am glad to boast about my weaknesses, so that the power of Christ may work through me." [1]

A thorn. A rock. We all trip over something.

If my weakness has any merit, at least it shows off his strength. If there is any benefit to my sin, at least it reminds me of how much I need God. After all, it's when I have fallen the hardest that I most appreciate his help. It's when I am desperate and hurt that his love feels the warmest.

It's when I am flat on my face that I realize most clearly both my condition and his provision.

If his power works best in my weakness, then he must be strong indeed.

When I was a kid, my mom planted a patch of mint in the side yard. I don't know if you've ever seen actual mint grow, but it looks like a weed. It looks like a weed, but it smells like tic-tacs. And when you're eleven years old and mowing the yard, it cuts down and shoots out of the little place where the cut grass shoots out of a lawnmower just like a weed. The thing about mint is, when you cut it back (and by "cut it back" I mean "mow it down"), it multiplies. And by multiplies I mean "invades your yard like a bunch of little minty-fresh Nazis until your entire yard smells like Santa's soul patch." We had the most refreshing yard on the block. Every time I cut the grass, it smelled like a Dentyne commercial. Thanks to me, every dog on our block peed Listerine.

Even when you mow mint down, it comes back. With a vengeance. Every time.

Just when I think I have my mess cleaned up and my faith figured out, it seems like the weeds come back. With a vengeance. As a wise man once said, "If you think you are standing firm, be careful that you don't fall." Again.

The weeds come back.

Fortunately, where sin multiplies, so does grace.

When Paul had a similar struggle, he said, "Oh what a miserable person I am! Who will free me from this life that is dominated by sin? Thank God! The answer is in Christ Jesus our Lord." [2]

I believe that answer, but my frustration is that while I have a relationship with Jesus, I don't feel like I have been set free from my sin. Not all of it. And it's the bit that keeps coming back that is really proving to be a problem. Maybe my expectations are too high. Jesus never promised that I wouldn't have to deal with the presence of my sin. He just promised that I wouldn't have to deal with the result of my sin.*

Paul asked, "Who will free me from this life that is dominated by sin? Thank God! The answer is in Christ Jesus our Lord."

His question was, "Who will free me?" Well, Jesus will. Sometime in the future. He will free me. One bright morning when this life is over, I'll fly away. I'll walk through a tunnel and into a bright light where I'll live in a place that isn't dominated by sin and temptation and insecurity and gossip and hurt feelings and revenge and divorce and anger and sadness and selfishness and confusion and lust and pornography and greed and poorly chosen words and inappropriate jokes and everything else that keeps me from being the man I was created to be. One day. He will free me. When this life is over.

**By "result," I mean "the ultimate result of my sin." I don't have to worry about the judgment of God for the ridiculous (and sometimes deliberate) mistakes I have made. Logic follows that I shouldn't have to worry about judging myself either. This doesn't mean, however, that I don't have to deal with some of the more practical and immediate results of my sin like damaged relationships, unpleasant memories, and poorly applied tattoos.*

But maybe not until then. Until then I still live in a fallen world where I have to deal with the temptation that surrounds me and the filth that I have filled myself with. I will one day be set free, but not for a while.

So what do I do until then? Until then I keep mowing the yard and doing my best.

Now there is no condemnation for those who belong to Christ Jesus. For the power of the life-giving Spirit has freed us through Christ Jesus from the power of sin that leads to death.[3]

In the future I will be free, but for now I get to enjoy the fact there is no condemnation for those of us who belong to Christ Jesus. No condemnation. I may still have to deal with the presence of my sin, but the consequences are taken care of. I may still feel temptation, but I don't have to worry about condemnation, fear, and judgment. That's a pretty decent trade. Today I can rest in the fact that the power of Jesus' love for me has freed me from the power of sin that leads to death.

I may not be free from the power of sin's attraction. I still have to wrestle with that. But I am free from the fact that its lure leads to the death of my soul and my ultimate separation from God. My freedom lies in my restored relationship with my God. I am pardoned. And he lets that be the end of it.

Thanks be to God.

Hi.

I am here to fill an empty hole.

Just like the Oscars.

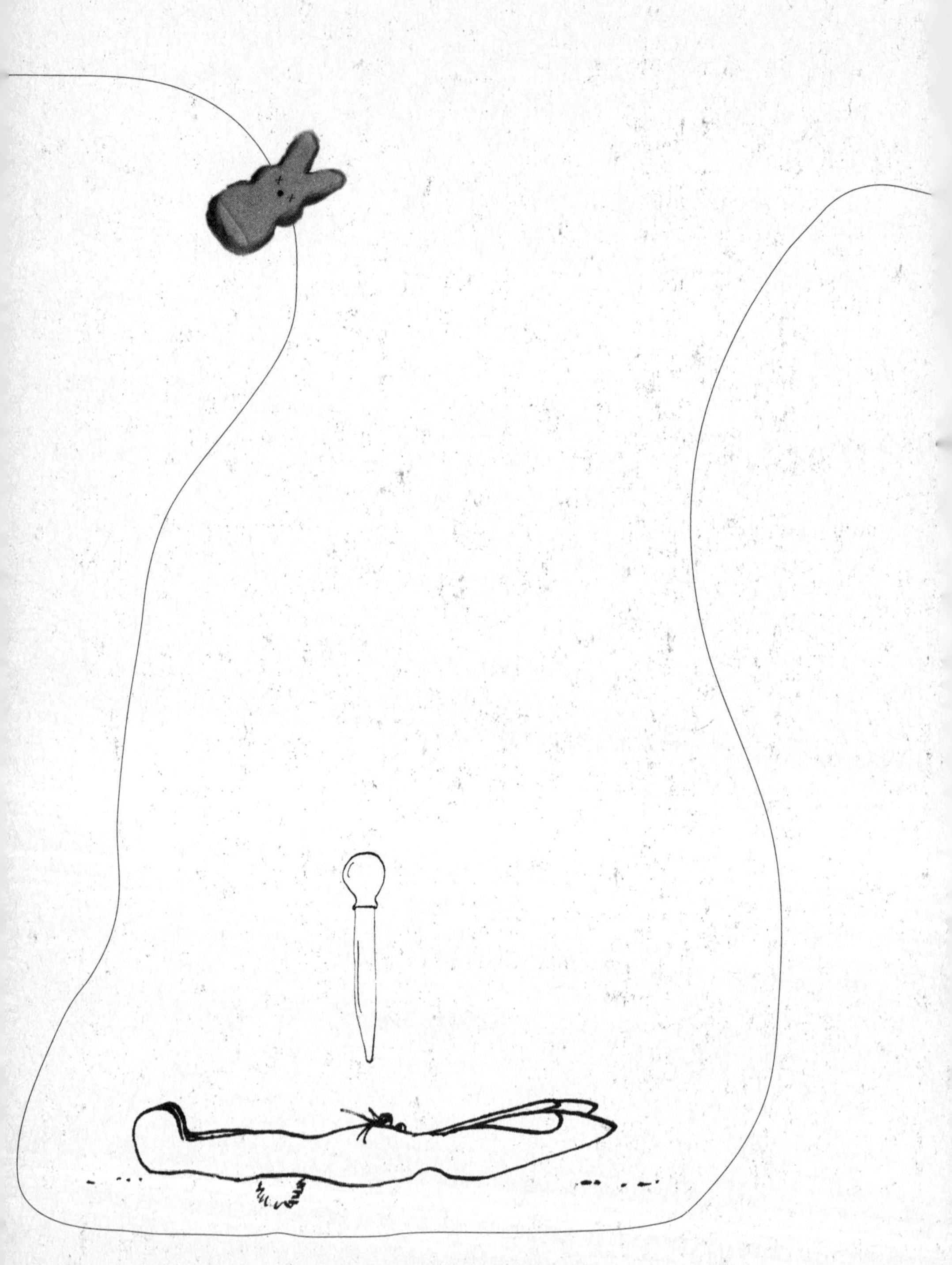

Dead Bunnies

I tried out a new church a couple of weeks ago. It's not that I'm not happy with my usual church or anything dramatic like that. I just needed a change. Sometimes you just need a change. So I woke up one Sunday, put on my good jeans, and went to a new church. I didn't sit in the back, but I was close. I just wanted to blend in. Sometimes you just want to blend in.

That seems to be a theme in my life. I didn't really want to see anybody I knew. I didn't want to talk about having lunch after. I didn't want to be recognized or welcomed or thanked. I didn't want to stand and greet my neighbor and pretend like I was thrilled about making a new friend. I just wanted to be in church and soak up whatever it is churches are supposed to be full of. In short, I guess I wanted to worship. I wanted my own private encounter with God.

I sat just as the band was beginning to play. I'll be honest and admit that as a long-time church person and kind of professional Christian, I feel like I've seen it all. I've heard all the songs and sermons. I've seen the lights and smoke and screens and projectors and and drama and dancers and hymns and choruses and organs and guitars and drums and choirs and sign language and blacklights and videos and puppets and object lessons. Once I even saw a guy preach an entire sermon from a canoe. I forget why. I've been in literally hundreds of churches and sat in worship services that have ranged in sophistication from Bill Gates to Barney Rubble. As a result I generally walk into worship pretty critically, with a red pen in my brain, reviewing it like the movie I saw the night before. I'm not easily impressed.

But this day was different. As the band started to play, I was impressed. They were good. They were more than good. They were really good. Since I live in Nashville, home of countless starving, struggling, and hopeful musicians, it's not unusual to go to church and hear quality music. But somehow this was different. I found myself sitting self-contained and absorbed by worship and music and art.

In one particularly powerful interlude, I heard the surprised critic in my brain say, "These guys are really outstanding. Innovative. Different. If they put out an album, I'd definitely buy it. They really should record and show the world how great they are. It's cliché for a worship band in Nashville to put out an album and sell it out front after church, but I don't care. I'd go out to the lobby right now and buy it and burn it and give it to my friends. That's how good they are. I'd happily spread their exceptional talent by stealing their music. They should seriously record an album."

I couldn't get enough.

And then it was over. The last song faded and the band shuffled out. They had done their job and now it was the preacher's turn. We sat. We listened. He was good also, but I was still silently engrossed by the fabulous sound this band had produced. I wanted more. They had become my four-count worship drug.

Thankfully, forty minutes later, after the preacher produced his five points, the musicians came back out for an encore. Of course, by "encore" I mean "closing worship set." But the two seem to be interchangeable when you sometimes confuse worship with music. Not that any of us would ever do that. Regardless, I was happy to see the band take the stage again. They didn't disappoint.

Still itching to buy these guys' imagined album and discover a new talent, I waited for the pastor's closing remarks before sprinting to the lobby to make my purchase. I'm glad I hesitated. His final sentence made me feel like a fool.

He closed by saying, "Thanks for coming. Blah … blah … blah. And we'd also like to thank our band, Jars of Clay, for leading us in worship this morning."

Our band, Jars of Clay.

That may not mean much to you. Your formative years might not have been super-saturated with Christian music like mine were. But if they were, you should recognize the name. In the mid-nineties you couldn't turn on your radio without hearing their hit single "Flood" on both Christian and mainstream stations. Every time I started my car, Jars of Clay told me that it hadn't stopped raining for days. Their world was a flood. Slowly they'd become one with the mud. That self-titled album now hangs on a studio wall somewhere dipped in double platinum, celebrating the fact that it sold more than two million copies. Congratulations. If you put that double platinum album next to their platinum album (*Much Afraid*), their gold album (*I Left the Zoo*), their three Grammy Awards, and their seventeen number-one singles, you've officially built a shrine to one of the most celebrated and innovative bands the Christian music industry has seen to date.

Jars of Clay has produced nine albums, which have sold more than five million copies over the past eleven years, and I own four of them.

In the Christian music world, they are a legend.

And I sat wishing they would put out an album.

I'm an idiot.

I was so desperate for what this band was giving me that I didn't recognize who they were or what they had already given me. I wanted to buy their music, but I already own their music. I wanted more, but I can listen to them any time I want. I wanted them to be famous — and therefore easily purchased and playable on my iPod —but I didn't realize that they are already famous and easily purchased and playable on my iPod.

I wanted the band to be accessible, but they're already accessible.

Jars of Clay should put out an album. That's about like the Easter Bunny telling Santa that he should buy some reindeer. Brilliant.

Jesus is the visible image of the invisible God. He is the famous one in our midst. He is God right in front of us. He not only made everything (both the things we can see and the things we cannot see) sometime in the past, but he also holds everything together in the present. He is our universal strength super glue. He is the One who sings all around us, even when we fail to recognize it.

He is the accessible God.

Jesus may have been clouded by preachers who have told us only about wrath and hell and judgment. He may have been forced to hide behind the priorities that we have put in front of him. My view of him may have even been blinded by the shame or guilt or carelessness of my own actions. But that doesn't mean he isn't here. Every time I experience something good and pure that makes my soul happy and content, I am in the presence of God.

I recently read in the Bible where it says that "God, in all his fullness was pleased to live in Christ, and by him God reconciled everything in heaven and on earth by means of his blood on the cross." [1]

The phrase "was pleased to live in Christ" stopped me. I had forgotten.

It made him happy.

In my opinion, this may be the craziest part of the whole human story. God, in all his fullness (not just his wrath and judgment and serious Old Testament self, but also his love and compassion and sense of humor) was pleased to live in Christ. God showed me how completely he understands me by becoming a person like me. A person who sweats, shouts, giggles, and cries. He didn't want to seem far away, the God carelessly spinning creation on his finger. So he wrapped himself in skin and hair and came close. Intimate. Happy to be a part of our drama.

God lived in Christ so that I could know he is present. Accessible. The God right in front of me. Singing even when I don't recognize it. Happy to be one of us.

He enjoyed coming down for a visit.

I think I often miss that part of the story. I sometimes get the impression that on the first Christmas night way back when, as Mary and Joseph were kickin' it in the manger and everybody else was wrapping presents and getting their last-minute shopping done, God was laid back in his chair watching *Seinfeld* reruns and trying to read the paper when he just grew tired of listening to all our noise.

"Fine!" he shouts. "Jesus, would you please just go take care of whatever it is those people need?"

And Jesus says, "Do I have to? I just got in from putting out the star. I really don't feel like going back out tonight."

"Fine!" God barks. "Do I have to do everything myself?"

And Jesus answers, "No, I'll go. Have you seen my swaddling clothes anywhere?"

I forget that when it all went down, the angels declared, "Good News!" Both heaven and earth were happy. It wasn't punishment. It was good news. It wasn't God simply doing his job. It was good news. It wasn't a baby. It was good news.

We talk so much about the sacrifice Jesus made in walking our dusty planet that I'm afraid we tend to miss that this was his choice. And he was pleased to do it.

When my mom was a little girl, my grandfather went hunting and found a huddle of newborn bunnies abandoned in the woods. Abandoned bunny babies. Could there be anything sadder? Apparently the Easter Bunny really isn't as responsible as we'd like to think he is. Either that or he's dead because my grandfather shot him on the hunt.

Regardless, Gran (that's what we called my grandfather) took the bunnies home to my mother and her brother and sister to keep as pets.

If you haven't seen a newborn bunny in a while, they aren't much more than little furballs with a hole in each end. Like small, albino Elmo droppings. My grandmother was saddled with the responsibility of "raising" the bunnies by feeding them milk with an eyedropper. But she couldn't figure out why every time she fed them, they coughed, sputtered, and sneezed. At every meal, tiny eruptions shook the bunnies' small bodies in fits and spasms. And then, nothing. Absolutely nothing. No movement. No suckling. No sneezing. Nothing.

That's because dead bunnies don't typically do much.

My Grandmother couldn't understand why the bunnies kept dying. I mean, that is pretty puzzling. She had been feeding her own children for years and had yet to encounter this problem. Surely bunny moms in the wild don't have this experience. Of course, bunny moms in the wild are not feeding their children with eyedroppers full of milk. They know what they're doing. They know how to feed their children. That's what bunny moms are made for. Hopping, carrot eating, egg dying, and baby bunny feeding.

Plus, bunny moms know that milk goes in the mouth, not up the nose.

My grandmother also knew that, but in the hair and small of it all, she just couldn't tell which hole was the nose and which hole was the mouth. And so the little bunny pets drowned, one eyedropper at a time. Every last one of them.

Talk about lactose intolerant.

Blessed are those who hunger and thirst for righteousness, for they will be filled. [2]

No wonder I feel so empty most of the time.

I'm glad my nose and mouth are not easily confused. I'm also glad my mother no longer has to make airplane noises to make me eat my vegetables. I have learned to feed myself. I'm independent. Able to take care of myself. Able to do for myself.

But just because I am independent doesn't mean that I'm responsible. Just because I can feed myself doesn't mean that I do it well. I know what my body needs to keep it alive, but I still eat junk. I know what my spirit needs to keep it healthy, but I feed it trash too. Or starve it beyond recognition.

Just because I know what I should do doesn't mean that I

do it. Just because I know what I should not do doesn't mean that I stop.

I'm independent. But maybe my independence is my downfall. It's the reason I feel so far away from God. The reason I feel separated. I am afraid I've convinced myself that I can do lots of things for myself that I was never meant to do. I was meant to pay my bills, fix my own dinner, earn a living, and take out the trash. These are basic life skills that even Adam and Eve would have mastered eventually. But there are certain needs that I was never meant to provide for myself.

I have needs for love, intimacy, affection, security, worth, and relationship that I am not capable of filling on my own. In the garden, God met these needs for Adam and Eve. In a perfect world, God provides these for me. But because sin entered the picture, I was separated from God and pushed out of the perfect garden and eventually into an American culture that has convinced me I am the master of my own domain. I am in control. I can provide for my own needs.

But I can't. Not the big ones. I've tried. It was disastrous.

My problem is that I'm feeding all the right hungers in all the wrong ways. And in the process I am choking myself. My hunger for sex is natural and right, but I find that I feed it in the wrong way. My hunger for success, accomplishment, and recognition is natural, but I feed it the wrong way. A hunger to be needed, appreciated, and loved was born inside me, but I tend to feed that in the wrong way too. That's why my sin is so tricky. I feel natural urges, but then I try to feed them in unnatural ways.

I try to do for myself what God was meant to do for me. Isn't that stubborn independence the root of my separation from him?

When I try to feed my deepest needs for relationship, acceptance, value, and happiness with the perversions that I find every day, I feel myself pushed further and further from God. I feel my soul choke.

These perversions separate me from God because in some mysterious way that I have yet to understand, God wants to meet my deepest needs for me. With something pure. Something right. Something that fits. And when I take over that responsibility, I am doing something I was never made to do. And I'm not very good at it. I'm clumsy and awkward. I make mistakes.

Those mistakes are killing me. One eyedropper at a time.

This includes you who were once so far away from God. You were his enemies, separated from him by your evil thoughts and actions, yet now he has brought you back as friends.[3]

That's my problem. Separation.

Once upon a time, a father fish was separated from his son. The son's name was Nemo. Maybe you've seen his movie.

One day Marlin decided it was time to give his son a taste of freedom, let him make a few of his own choices. It was a dangerous idea, and Marlin was not completely comfortable with it, but what's a fish to do? You can't keep the big ocean a secret forever. So, despite his fear, the father fish let his son go to school. And on the very first day of school, Nemo went with his class on a field trip to the drop-off. The drop-off. Where the reef ends and freedom begins. The watery edge of Eden.

As they gazed into the mystifying blue, Nemo and his friends saw a boat. A boat. Nemo had never seen a boat before. His friends dared him to swim past the safety of the reef and into open water. And he did. After all, danger is an enticing idea for a sheltered clownfish. So Eve … I mean Nemo … made a choice to exercise his independence and go where he had never gone before. And even though his dad saw him swimming into the deep and yelled for him to stop, Nemo kept swimming. Nemo kept swimming all the way to the boat. And when he got there, he touched it.

Nemo touched the boat because Nemo was being a brat. And he got caught. He got caught by a big, bad dentist who whisked him away from his father to live in a tank with a bunch of fishy freaks.

Why did Marlin tell Nemo to stop swimming and stay away from the boat? To protect his son? Yes. But Marlin was concerned with more than just his Nemo's safety. He didn't want Nemo to cross the drop-off because he didn't want his son to leave. He didn't want Nemo to go away. He didn't want to be separated from the child that he loved.

The rule was given to maintain a relationship.

But Nemo broke the rule, and his family was torn apart. His disobedience did not mean that Nemo didn't love his dad or that his dad didn't love him. But it did mean that father and son were separated. And something had to be done to bring them back together. They had to be reconciled.

So Marlin went looking for his son. Not because he had

to. Because he wanted to. He went all the way to 42 Wallaby Way, Sydney, Australia. And along the way he met a forgetful fish named Dori, several sharks, a few cool turtles, some seagulls, a pelican, and a few other friends.

Marlin did all of this because he wanted to restore a relationship with his son. He could have given up. But he didn't. He didn't give up because Nemo needed to be brought back. Reconciled. Marlin didn't wait for his son to figure out his mistake and solve his own problem. He went looking.

And he was pleased to do it.

The problem with my sin isn't that it's immoral. God doesn't hate my sin because it disappoints him. Disappointment requires surprise. And God isn't surprised by anything I do. The problem with my sin is that it destroys a relationship. Any rules that God has chosen to give haven't been to hold me back or even just to protect me. They've been given to maintain a relationship. They've been given because he doesn't want me to lose my innocence. He doesn't want me to go away.

I have been taught that God hates my sin because it keeps me from having a relationship with him. But that doesn't always bother me like it should. When I am absorbed in my own life and enjoying my disobedience, I don't always care about the state of my relationship with God. And that's definitely a problem. But I really think God hates my sin because it keeps him from having a relationship with me. It keeps *him* from having a relationship with *me*. And he wants that relationship even when I don't.

That's why the cross is so beautiful for those of us who follow Christ. The cross is God reconciling me. Coming to find me. Bringing me back as his friend. The cross is Jesus making peace with everything in heaven and on earth by means of his blood.

And he was pleased to do it. Not to judge the world or get history back on track or to get his name on a bumper sticker, but to restore a relationship. To reconcile us. To find Nemo.

I was at a writer's conference recently trying to brainstorm ways that a certain organization could teach several thousand teenagers how they can live revolutionary lives for God. Our creative brain-tank was split into two groups. The task of my group was to develop an outline that would communicate how an average person can experience spiritual revolution. In roughly thirty minutes.

To be honest, I have a hard time trusting any three-point plan that claims it can revolutionize my life and spirituality in thirty minutes. There's a reason why movies are becoming longer and the half-hour situation comedy is dying. Nobody really believes anything can be solved between two commercial interruptions. But I was willing to try.

I suggested to the group that we look at the Old Testament book of Judges. A few Sundays earlier I was reminded by a pastor of what a dramatic pattern the book of Judges presents of ancient Israel's experience with God. Studying their experience was like looking in a mirror at the past twelve years of my own life. Spooky. In the book of Judges there are about thirteen cycles where . . .

The people rebel against God.

The people are disciplined by a God who cares for them.

The people apologize and attempt to change.

The people are reconciled (or brought back) through a "judge."

And then the people rebel again.

When I mentioned this to our facilitator as a possible starting point for our discussion of spiritual revolution, he responded, "But the people always rebel again. Can we really teach people that we always rebel again?"

I responded, "That has been my experience. Has it not been yours?"

Apparently I don't have a very successful spirituality.

The outline our group landed on looked something like this …

Point 1. Realize we're broken. (We are people who have fallen short of what we were created to be.)

Point 2. Realize we can be fixed. (God doesn't give up on us in our brokenness.)

Point 3. Realize we can stay fixed. (For this point the group agreed a prescription of Bible Study, regular prayer, and time spent with people of faith is what is needed for a believer to "stay fixed.")

I realize, sometimes with too much clarity, that I'm broken. I am infinitely thankful that I can be fixed and forgiven. But all day I stewed over the idea that I can *stay fixed*. Our facilitator thought the idea was brilliant. I'm not so sure.

My experience is that I don't stay fixed very well. I read my Bible. I pray. I spend time with other believers. But I'm still broken. I still swear and lust and do a great many things that I'm not brave enough to write on this page. I will always be in a relationship with Jesus. I will always be loved. For some unbelievable reason I will always be forgiven. But I will probably not stay fixed.

This is not a comment on God's ability to do the repair. I just know myself well enough to know that no matter which way I turn, I cannot always make myself do right. I want to, but I can't. When I want to do good, I don't. Sometimes when I try not to do wrong, I do it anyway.

And when I try to fix myself, even if it is with a very careful prescription of prayer, Bible study, and time spent with fellow believers, I find that I still end the day broken.

I will always be broken. I will always need to be brought back. I will always need a redeemer because I will always want my sin. That's what's broken about me. As I understand it, an alcoholic never stops wanting alcohol. He just learns how to deal with his desire. That's why he keeps going to the meetings. He will always be broken. He will always need to be fixed. He will always need to be reconciled. He will always need to be brought back to the person he was meant to be.

I am selfish. I don't always choose the things I love over the things God loves, but I have. And I will again. And probably again after that. The weeds will always return. I will continue to try to fix and feed myself in the wrong ways and choke in the process. I don't have to be happy about it, but I find that I beat myself up a whole lot less when I accept that this is who I am. I am a broken man. The sooner I come to realize this, the less guilt I'll feel and the more grace I'll understand.

I will always need to be fixed. But I don't need to be fixed as much as I need to be brought back. Brought back to the accessible God. Reconciled.

Fortunately, it will please him to do it.

1
1

Uno

In high school I dated the same girl for about three and a half years. She was amazing.

Our love affair started the first day of our freshman year during our first period class. Latin. I don't know if dead languages invite romance or if the naked marble woman on the cover of our textbook sparked my imagination, but the first day of high school turned out to be pretty memorable. It was the day I met my first love. We'll call her Laura.

I sat patiently waiting for class to start when the most beautiful creature I had ever seen walked through the door. Actually, she didn't walk as much as she floated. Not like one of those gigantic balloons in the Thanksgiving Day parade. She wasn't so huge that she had to be tethered to the ground. No, she floated like a delicate feather on the breeze. She floated with long, dark hair that bounced when she moved. Her eyes were as deep and blue as Nemo's drop-off. Her skin glowed like the dawn. And she smelled like every boy's best dream.

She was a girl. Breathtaking. When Laura walked through

the door, I swear the heavens opened and angels sang. Laura reminded me why God spoke creation and said that it was good. She was a vision. I needed her to be mine.

So I prayed. "God, if you love me at all, you will cause this goddess to sit in front of me. Please," I begged. It worked. She sat.

I couldn't believe it. God was indeed good and real and listening to me. I was listening to my hormones, but God was listening to me. This perfect specimen of feminine beauty sat a few short inches in front of me. I couldn't control myself. Nervous energy pulsed through my body as spiking testosterone levels clouded both mind and judgment. My heart raced. My palms sweated. It's wonderful to be a pubescent teenage boy.

As I nervously swung my short ninth-grade legs beneath my seat, though, I failed to realize that each swing caused me to kick the back of her desk. I didn't realize it, that is, until this vision turned fully around in her chair and glared at me. With daggers shooting out of those beautiful blue eyes, she barked, "Would you *please* stop kicking the back of my chair?"

It was the voice of an angel.

I was in love.

In the weeks to come, Laura and I actually spoke to each other, and friendship eventually bloomed into something more. It was a match made in heaven and grown in the fertile soil of our high school hearts. As it turned out, we not only had first period Latin together, but we also sat next to each other during fifth period English. At our school every English class was required to learn an appreciation for Shakespeare by reading one of his plays. Freshmen had to read the classic *Romeo and Juliet*. I don't care how awkward your teenage years are/were, if you can't manage to woo a woman while reading *Romeo and Juliet*, you have serious problems.

I did not have serious problems.

At the end of the first term, our English teacher brought an old movie version of the play for us to watch during class. What a wonderful idea. As Mrs. Whateverhernamewas turned off the lights, I scooted my desk closer to Laura's under the pretense of needing a better view. Like an expert fisherman trolling the waters of love, I let my right hand dangle casually over the edge of the armrest, hoping for the best. Laura took the bait and allowed her hand to brush mine. It was a magical moment. I was certain that everyone in the room must have felt the electricity. They couldn't have avoided seeing the spark. The room felt warm, and so did I. So we sat for an entire act with our hands just touching. Touching. Nothing more. It was paradise.

I didn't know what to do next.

Eventually, in a moment of bravery and unbridled passion, my little finger crossed hers and we sat holding pinkies. Pinkies. It was nauseatingly wonderful. By the time the star-crossed lovers on screen made their fatal mistake and died in each other's arms, Laura and I were sitting with all five of our fingers interlocked, holding hands the boyfriend-girlfriend way. Intertwined. Unbreakable. Life could be no sweeter.

Laura and I would continue to date until our senior year when I dumped her. We broke up for several reasons. One of the most significant was that I came to realize that she did not know how to spell. Maybe that's too picky a reason to break up with someone, but sometimes spelling counts.

You see, relatively early in our relationship Laura and I had proclaimed our unending love for each other. But it wasn't until senior year that I became aware of her spelling disability. While the rest of the world spelled the word *love* the traditional L-O-V-E way, Laura chose to spell it another way. W-H-E-N.

Yep, sometimes spelling counts.

Laura was always telling me she loved me. But her body language (and sometimes lack thereof), constant mood shifting, and unpredictable emotions communicated something different. Instead of a simple, "Bryan, I love you," she chose to express, "Bryan, I love you when ..."

... You take me out.

... You tell me I'm beautiful.

... You buy me nice presents.

... You don't act like an idiot.

... I feel like it.

When I missed one of the requirements, Laura turned to her secret girl weapon. The power pout. And the force was strong in her family.

Dating Laura was like dating a deck of Uno cards. The rules kept changing and I kept losing and I couldn't figure out why. It drove me crazy because I wanted to love her and I wanted her to love me, but I couldn't figure out the rules. She was wearing me out. So I got out.

I want to love God and I want God to love me, but sometimes I have a hard time figuring out the rules and living by the requirements. But as I've read the Bible for myself, I have discovered that God never says, "I love you *when* . . . ." He only says, "I love you." Not, "I love you when you do . . ." or, "I love you when you don't . . . ."

Just "I love you."

When I see the "rules" in the Bible, it becomes pretty clear they're not there for me to follow so I can be loved by God. They are not a condition of his feelings for me. They are there because my obedience demonstrates my love. I choose to live within his boundaries because I understand that every relationship has parameters, not because I'm afraid of what will happen when I step out of line. By living within these parameters, I show that I'm committed to trusting God's love for me.

I live in a world where I've learned that I must earn what I want. Nothing good is free. Nothing worthwhile happens without effort. I worked to get good graces. Now I work to get a paycheck. I work to win a game. I work to get a girlfriend. I work to get a raise. I work to get a promotion. I work. I have been taught that any good I receive in life I get because I have earned it.

But I do not earn God's love. On some level I find this inconceivable. Not just that I don't have to earn God's love. But that I *cannot* earn God's love. Even when I try, I just can't.

I generally try to live a good moral life because I think that's what I have to do for God to love me. To be proud of me. To not be angry with me. But that's the miracle. Even when I am good and moral, I haven't impressed God. I cannot impress God. I have not earned his love, but he has given it to me anyway. For everything else there's MasterCard. But this is priceless.

God is so rich in mercy, and he loved us so very much, that even while we were dead because of our sins, he gave us life when he raised Christ from the dead. [1]

I think this may be God's greatest proof that I am valuable to him. I have been given a gift I didn't deserve and a love I cannot earn. God doesn't love me because of what I do on the outside. He doesn't love me because I read the Bible, pray a lot, or try to love other people. He loves me even when I don't do those things. God doesn't love me because of what I don't do on the outside. He doesn't love me just because I try not to swear, fight, or look at dirty movies. He loves me even when I do those things. God is so rich in mercy and he loved me so very much that even while I was dead because of my sin, he gave me life. God doesn't even love me because of who I am on the inside. He doesn't love me because I try to be spiritual or moral or because I've "given my heart to him." He loves me even when I'm not spiritual or moral or surrendering myself to him.

He doesn't love me when. He just loves me.

God loves me by nature of the fact that he made me. There's nothing I can do to earn it. There's nothing I can do to stop earning it. That's why I am safe in his love. I am loved just because I am.

I think that's why the Bible says, "God saved you by his special favor when you believed. And you can't take credit for this; it is a gift from God. Salvation is not a reward for the good things we have one, so none of us can boast about it." [2]

Whether we admit it or not, many of us are convinced that God really loves us (or loves us most) when we are doing and thinking right. We "feel" it when we're worshiping at our church or serving on a mission trip or enjoying some sort of moral victory. When we're proud of ourselves, we assume God must be proud of us too. When it's easy for me to love myself, I assume that it must be easier for God to love me too.

The problem with that logic is that when I'm not good, when I have a hard time loving me, I begin to believe that God must have a hard time loving me too. I begin to think that he only loves me when.

Some of us have heard, "For all have sinned and fallen short of the glory of God" so many times and are so convinced that God cannot tolerate our sin that we are also convinced God cannot tolerate us when we are sinful and that he would never put our picture on his fridge. And as much as we sing and talk about the great love God gives to even the most unworthy of people, we're not convinced this love is for us too.

When I fall, I feel that my sin separates me from God and I hate that. But what I really hate is that when I cross the line and really screw up, I'm afraid I've stopped earning God's love. Maybe now I've even earned his hate. I'm afraid that when I'm dirty and broken I'm not valuable anymore. I feel lost and unlovable, separated from God and his creation. And I look around at all those other people out there who seem to have it all figured out, and I say to myself, "There's no way I'm as loved as they are. There's no way I'm as valuable as they are. I just can't be." But consider this:

When we were utterly helpless, Christ came at just the right time and died for us sinners. Now, no one is likely to die for a good person, though someone might be willing to die for a person who is especially good. But God showed his great love for us by sending Christ to die for us while we were still sinners. And since we have been made right in God's sight by the blood of Christ, he will certainly save us from God's judgment. For since we were restored to friendship with God by the death of his Son while we were still enemies, we will certainly be delivered from eternal punishment by his life. [3]

Do me a favor. If you skipped that last paragraph because you recognized it's from the Bible and/or you memorized these words forever ago and think you can afford to skip what you already know, go back and underline every phrase that tells you when God most loved you. I think you might be surprised.

Several years ago I worked for a large Christian camp in North Carolina where I taught an eighth-grade Bible study. I love eighth graders, but you can't get around the fact that watching a room full of eighth-grade boys is very much like going to the zoo. During feeding time. This is due, in large part, to the fact that an eighth-grade boy is a human eating machine. He is a garbage disposal with a face. And the more he eats, the more he grows. In fact, they say that if you can get an eighth-grade boy to stand still long enough, you can actually watch him grow taller. I'm not sure if that's true. I've never seen one stand still that long.

Eighth-grade boys are like something from the Sci Fi Channel. They have this mysterious grow juice pulsing through their bodies and turning them into men. They grow four inches every twenty-five minutes, and their pants never fit. Their shoes are always too small. And for some reason they smell like wet goats. At the zoo. I love them, but it's true.

But there is a brief moment of peace before this happens. There is a calm before the storm when the grow juice has not yet started to pump and your boy is still only four feet high and has to reach up to hold his girlfriend's hand. If he holds his girlfriend's hand. It's a well-established fact that girl hands carry cooties. That's why eighth-grade boys regularly get "the shot." Regardless, it was our first day at camp with a fresh batch of students when this amazing eighth-grader named Kyle walked into my Bible study room. He was still in the calm before the growing storm.

As he walked in, I looked at his nametag and said, "Hey, Kyle, how's it going?" It was a standard question, and he gave a standard answer: "Fine." But when he did, it was unlike anything I had ever heard before. The voice that came out of this small, innocent, four-foot-tall body sounded like Darth Vader with a cold. He was twelve years old with the voice of a forty-five-year-old chain smoker. I was jealous. I am thirty and still get called "m'am" on the phone.

So as Kyle went to grab a chair, I almost said out loud, "Dude, if your body ever catches up with your voice, you are going to be unstoppable. You will be a living, breathing Incredible Hulk. Or maybe Bigfoot. Or Barry White."

But there was one other thing that made Kyle different. Not only was he four feet tall with the voice of a John Deere tractor, he also had a large purple birthmark that covered the left side of his face.

That night I stood at the door of the camp auditorium with my friend Julie greeting kids as they walked into the worship gathering. As Kyle came through the door I gave him a high five. My hand was at approximately belly-button height. Kyle had to reach up to hit it. When he did, Julie bent down and said, "Well, hello Kyle" in a voice covered in cotton candy. During the non-summer months Julie was a second-grade school teacher. But she wasn't the second grade teacher that you hated. She was the really nice one that smelled good and gave you free homework passes on your birthday and made you feel all tingly inside.

You know the one.

When Julie saw the purple mark on Kyle's face she said, "Kyle, what happened to your face?"

I froze, mortified. How could she say such a thing? Couldn't she see that this poor boy had a disfiguring birthmark? But fortunately the lobby was loud and people were passing by and there was music inside and Kyle didn't hear what she said.

So Kyle looked up at her and asked, "What?" He sounded like a lawnmower starting.

"You're face! What happened to your face?" Apparently Julie thought Kyle had been hit by a basketball or something.

Again Kyle responded, "What?" I think he may have been gargling rocks.

Frustrated, Julie raised her voice to be heard over the crowd and screamed, "YOUR FACE, KYLE! WHAT HAPPENED TO YOUR FACE?"

It was at that moment I realized this horrible conversation could go one of two ways. Kyle was either going to burst into tears and run up the mountain never to be seen again, or he was going to punch Julie in the throat.

But Kyle looked right at Julie, like she had a duck on her head, and said, "I don't know." He uttered this unbelievable phrase as if to say, "Look, I really don't have any idea what you're talking about. What do you mean, 'What happened to my face?' What happened to your face? And why are you talking to me? I don't know you."

And then Kyle trotted off into the auditorium like a little chain-smoking leprechaun.

As the week wore on, I came to understand why Kyle had acted so oblivious that night. He didn't tell Julie what was wrong with his face because there was nothing wrong with his face. It had a big spot that was a different color, but that was all. Kyle still saw with his eyes and smelled with his nose. His mouth still chewed and smiled. He was a perfectly wonderful, happy, and surprisingly secure eighth-grader. Kyle had learned to look past his imperfections and see his own potential.

I suspect this was because someone in Kyle's young life had had the wisdom to say to him, "Look Kyle, it doesn't matter that you're only four feet tall. Someday you could be the limbo champion of the world. It doesn't matter that your voice is three notes deeper than God's — think of the money you might make someday doing the voiceover for an orc in a *Lord of the Rings* movie. Kyle, it doesn't matter that your face is different from everyone else's, God doesn't look at outward appearance. God looks at the heart. And someday the trumpet will shout and we'll all be given new bodies and all this will be over anyway."

Apparently Kyle heard that and let it sink in. He actually believed that God looks past who we are now, the things that we think now and the things that we do now, and he looks into what we could become. Someday.

And I believe that too, but it's hard. It's hard because I honestly don't care about someday. I don't want people to love me for who I could potentially be. I want others to love me for who I am. I care about now. I want to know right now that I'm valuable. I want to know right now that I an worth something. I want right now for people to see how special, unique, individual, valuable, talented, smart, deep, and free thinking I am.

I don't want for anybody to have to look past anything. I want to be loved as I am. Right now.

God doesn't look past my sin and love me anyway. He looks into my sin and loves me, period. He doesn't say, "One day you'll be better, so I'll put up with you now." I'm not a piece of yard sale furniture that has great potential but needs to be fixed up a bit. While we were still sinners Christ died for us.

No one is likely to die for a good person, though someone might be willing to die for a person who is especially good. But God showed his great love for us by sending Christ to die for us while we were still sinners. [4]

While we were still sinners. The evidence isn't that God loves me in spite of my sin. The evidence is that God loves me in the midst of my sin. As I am. Right now.

He loves me even when I don't.

When I was in the eighth grade, I wasn't very popular. I was a fat kid. I know it's not politically correct to say "fat kid," but when you were one, I think you've earned the right to label yourself however you choose. My jeans tried to tell me that I was just husky, but I knew better. They were only trying to be nice. I knew that they didn't like the sight of my fat butt any more than I did. People would ask what I wanted to do when I grew up, and the only answer that seemed to fit was "eat pie." At the age of thirteen my best friend was a brownie, and we spent lots of time together.

And so I became known as "the funny fat kid." But at my school you didn't want to be the funny fat kid. Funny and fat weren't cool. For some reason the cool kids in my school were the ones who looked pretty and dressed right and had absolutely no personality of their own. I'm not saying that's true everywhere. But it was at my school.

One of the cool kids was named Pancho. Pancho was named after a Mexican revolutionary. He was skinny and he was cool and he was popular. And I was just like him. Except I wasn't skinny, I wasn't cool, I wasn't popular, and I wasn't Mexican. In other words, we had nothing in common.

One day I sat next to Pancho in computer class. For some reason the would-be revolutionary decided to take a step down the middle school food chain and talk to me. And I made him laugh. I made him laugh so hard that he spewed milk out of his nose, and he wasn't even drinking milk. I thought I was finally in. Then at the end of class, Pancho turned to me and said in his most flattering voice, "Ya know, Bryan, you'd be pretty cool … if you weren't so fat."

If you weren't so fat. He really thought he was paying me a compliment. Pancho was an idiot.

So for the next five years I did everything I could to be skinny so that I would be good enough to be cool. And about five years after I got skinny, I heard that Pancho had been arrested and sent to prison. As far as I know, Pancho is still behind bars being cool and skinny and making new friends with names like Buzzsaw, Killer, and Sweetheart.

I should probably feel guilty about the fact that I grinned while typing that sentence.

But I don't.

Pancho sold me the idea that people would love and like me only if I could measure up to a certain standard. Their standard. And I bought it. But that idea is poison.

When I begin to believe that people will only love me when I fit a certain mold, then I eventually also believe that God will only love me when I fit a certain mold. And I end up either busting my hump to measure up to that standard, or I give up altogether because I realize that I will never measure up. If I don't give up, if I live my life chasing my tail and trying to be good enough, there eventually comes a day when I realize that I'll never measure up to this imagined standard and become terrified that God loves me less because of it.

But what if there is no standard for being loved by God? What if God doesn't love good people any more than he loves bad people? What if God doesn't love bad people any less than good people? What if he just loves people? What if God loves Saddam Hussein as much as he loves Billy Graham? What if he loves Billy Graham as much he loves gay people? What if he loves gay people as much as he loves my pastor?

What if he loves my pastor as much as he loves the prostitutes downtown? What if he loves those prostitutes as much as he loves the Pope? What if he loves the Pope as much as he loves me? You get the idea. What if God just loves people? I'm not saying that he approves of all of these people's actions or is necessarily proud of them. You can love someone without being proud of them or approving of what they do.

What if God doesn't just love me when?

What if it really is true that God showed his great love for us in that while we were still sinners he died for us?

That's the scandal of Jesus. God doesn't just love people who are good enough. And that's good news because if he did, none of us would be good enough. God doesn't play favorites. If he did, it would be eighth grade all over again, and I'd still be the fat kid being picked last for dodgeball.

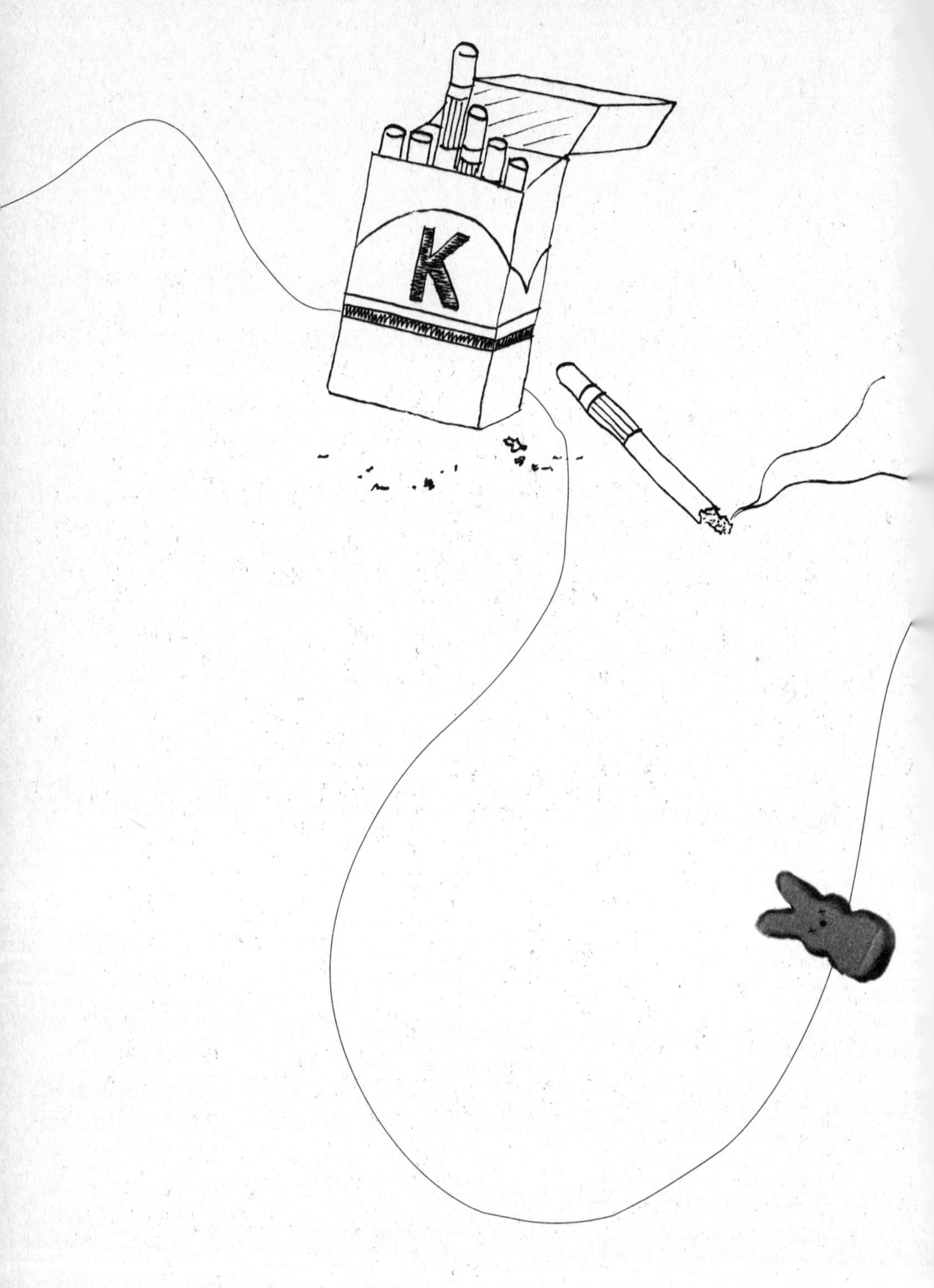
K

Kooter with a K

There is a bird who is trying to knock my house down. He has been trying for more than a year now. I am thankful he has not yet succeeded.

I live in a condo with a small, bricked back porch. My porch is my haven. It is twelve square feet of outdoors that I call my own. It is my fresh air and sunshine. It is my sanity when the indoors become too cluttered and too small.

My neighbor has a bush-like tree that stretches over the privacy fence separating our porches. Her tree produces bright red berries in the winter that fall onto my porch and decorate it for Christmas. By spring the Christmas berries have dried and shriveled into Easter raisins. This would not happen if I ever swept my porch. But I never sweep my porch. Maybe one day the Easter bunny will grow tired of eggs and chocolate and want raisins for a change. He is welcome to mine.

Spring is the one time of year when everybody still feels good about themselves. New Year's resolutions haven't been totally wasted. The days are nice enough to wear T-shirts, but we don't yet have to worry about bathing suits and all they will reveal. The trees in our backyards begin to get dressed, and the air feels clean with life and love. In the spring the robins come back. They enjoy being outside almost as much as I do. I don't intentionally feed them, but the birds flock to my porch and seem to enjoy the winter's leftover berries.

They also like attacking my house.

There is a sliding glass door that opens from my living room onto the porch. While the birds feast, they can look up and see their reflections in the glass. Most of the birds seem to enjoy the company. Stephen prefers to eat alone.

I have named one particular robin Stephen because of how much he seems to hate his own reflection. His namesake is a human friend of mine who claims that he hasn't looked in a mirror in ten years because the sight of his own face makes him uncomfortable.

There is nothing wrong with Stephen's face. All of the holes are in the right places, and none of them drip or drool excessively. He just does not like to look at his reflection. In department stores he turns away from the mirrors that are meant to help you decide which clothes to buy. He never uses his car's rearview mirror and avoids shiny things altogether. I don't know how he shaves without cutting off his lips. I don't think that he's a vampire, but I am honestly not sure. At least he doesn't attack the mirror. At least not that I know of.

But Stephen the bird does.

Every morning at 7:30 while Stephen is enjoying his breakfast of berries, he looks up to see himself reflected in my door. But instead of turning away or nonchalantly checking his hair like the rest of us do, he becomes angry. He becomes angry and attacks the glass.

When this started about a year ago, I heard the tapping and thought someone was knocking on my door needing to come in or wanting to sell me something. But then I saw the feathers and flapping and realized that a bird was pecking at my door. I took it to be a highly spiritual moment, a good omen, and wondered what the bird wanted, what he was trying to tell me. Did he want to be my friend? Did he think that I had something good to eat in my refrigerator? Would we form an everlasting bond that Disney would make into a movie based on the story of our lives together?

But then the pecking didn't stop.

I now wake to the sporadic rhythm of Stephen's beak tapping the glass of my back door. It's so predictable that I have stopped setting the alarm. Stephen gets me up in the morning. And the tapping goes on for hours. From 7:30 to 11:30 every spring morning, he pitches a little birdie fit by attacking his own reflection. Peck. Peck. Peck. He takes a break and gives me a reprieve until sunset. Then the pecking begins again.

It's like living in a telegraph station. I sometimes wonder if his relentless pecking is Morse code or if I should respond with something clever like, "Not by the hair of my chinny, chin, chin!" Or maybe Timmy has fallen into the well again. Stupid Timmy. When will he ever learn?

This happens every spring, throughout the summer, and into early fall. It's maddening. The constant peck, peck, pecking is making me insane. I really believe the kamikaze bird is trying to knock my house down.

I would enjoy Stephen much more if he weren't so self-destructive. Sometimes I too wake up in the morning and dread looking at myself in the mirror. But I don't throw a tantrum while brushing my teeth. Some days, like Stephen, I want to bang my head against the wall until the world goes dim. But it only takes one good whack before I realize there's a reason those eighties hair bands took so many drugs. Head banging hurts. But Stephen doesn't seem to care. He attacks himself for hours.

Last year the constant pecking drove me so crazy that I bought three Napoleon Dynamite posters and taped them to the door, hoping the unusual teenager would lend his unique personality and charm to the scarecrow business. Unfortunately, Napoleon was about as effective at scarecrowing as his Wizard of Oz cousin. I actually heard Stephen laughing once as he pecked at Napoleon's eyes.

I have even thought about shooting the pesky robin, but I'm not sure my neighbors would approve of this solution since it places them directly in the line of my sniper fire. Plus, a church sits on the hill directly behind my house. Its cross-topped steeple peeks down into my courtyard. As I plot Stephen's demise, I can almost hear their congregation singing "His Eye Is on the Sparrow." I don't think I could shoot a bird when I know He's watching me.

I have also contemplated poisoning a few of Stephen's precious berries, but I can't decide if this is a good idea. I have a can of roach spray under my kitchen sink. I could easily spray a few of the berries and scatter the poisoned fruit for birdie to eat with his breakfast. After all, if it is moral to poison a roach, why would it not be okay to poison a bird? Just because Stephen has a beautiful singing voice doesn't mean that he is above the law. In this country, only money, fame, and a successful athletic career give you that privilege.

But with my luck Stephen would eat the tainted berries and they wouldn't kill him. He would just get an upset stomach and have explosive bird diarrhea all over my porch. Plus, when Snow White ate the poisoned apple, didn't seven angry dwarfs attack the evil queen and push her off a cliff? Stephen I can deal with. The last thing I need is an army of small bearded men knocking down my door.

And so the kamikaze bird continues to crash into my house.

I wish this story had a happy ending. I wish it ended with my making a new little birdie friend who fills my day with endless song. But Stephen does not fill my day with song. He fills it with irritation. He starts my mornings by banging his head against the door. He's a percussionist with no rhythm, and he's driving me crazy.

A happy ending would be nice, but I would even settle for a sad ending to Stephen's story. I've read *Where the Red Fern Grows*. I've seen *Pet Cemetery*. Should the worst happen, I would know what to do.

I just want the madness to end. And I think Stephen does too. Surely he cannot enjoy attacking his reflection for hours on end. And when he finally goes home at night, his feathers a tousled mess, I wonder if Mrs. Stephen believes him when he says, "Not tonight, honey. I have a headache."

Poor Stephen is trapped. There are no bars, ceilings, or gates, but still he's trapped. He has been given all of the world in which to fly, but he has chosen to imprison himself on my porch. I assume he goes home every night to his little robin family, but every day is spent endlessly focusing on himself. Trapped by his own reflection. One day this fascination will kill him. He'll hit his head too hard, and it will all be over. The pecking will end, and I'll finally be able to sleep past 7:30. But it hasn't ended.

All because Stephen can't take his eyes off the reflection and focus on the freedom of an endless sky.

Sadly, I am also trapped. I have been given an entire world of beauty, music, art, passion, laughter, and love in which to soar. But I am trapped in a prison with no bars. Like Stephen I have become fixated on myself. I have chosen to let myself become a prisoner to my computer, to food, to work, to what other people think of me, to what my body wants from me, to my bank account, and to an endless number of other pursuits that have taken my eye off the beauty of the world around me, encouraging me to focus on me.

I have been given the freedom to fly, but instead I've chosen a smaller existence. An existence that focuses on me. And most days, I feel like I'm banging my head against the glass.

I live a kamikaze life.

I have become convinced that the illusion is real. I've convinced myself that I really am the most important thing in my world. I've convinced myself that focusing on my own desires will end up making my life a better, happier place. But in the end, it's madness. A glass door. The trash I download to make myself happy only leaves me wanting more. The bank account that is supposed to make my life more comfortable is a pit that never fills. The reputation I've built that is supposed to earn respect or security or make me feel better about myself just makes me more neurotic about other people's opinions.

I am frustrated by how small my life has become. How limited my vision. How controlled my passions. How stale my creativity. How forced my laughter. How insecure and out of control I am in the private places of my soul.

This world was meant to be my haven. My fresh air and sunshine. My sky and freedom. But I'm trapped on a porch, staring at my own reflection in the glass, wondering why my head hurts.

And one day I fear this fascination will kill me.

In its purest form, the sin that the Bible warns me against is little more than a fascination with self. My most destructive and spiritually damaging behavior generally begins with me focusing too much on me.

The Bible unpacks this truth with wisdom and poetry. It says, "Those who are dominated by the sinful nature think about sinful things, but those who are controlled by the Holy Spirit think about things that please the Spirit. If your sinful nature controls your mind, there is death. But if the Holy Spirit controls your mind there is life and peace. For the sinful nature is always hostile to God. It never did obey God's laws, and it never will." [1]

The word here that has been translated "sinful nature" literally means "flesh." "Those who are dominated by the *flesh* think about things of the *flesh*." But the word *flesh* seems so small. Flesh is what covers bones and is scraped when we fall off a bike. Flesh is what has been glued together to form our bodies. Flesh is so basic. So primitive. So unspiritual.

And so appropriate.

Our flesh is what is left when we strip away our spiritual component. To say that those who are dominated by the flesh (sinful nature) think about things of the flesh (sinful things) is to say that those who concentrate on the body will be controlled by the body. Those who focus on themselves will be controlled by themselves.

I have not had much luck controlling myself in the past.

Those who live according to the flesh (sinful nature) have their mind set on what that nature desires. And what does my flesh desire? What does my selfish nature desire? It desires whatever makes me happy in the moment. It has little regard for consequences, little regard for the lessons I've learned in the past, little regard for the other people in my life, and little regard for the ultimate goals God and I have for the future.

It desires sex rather than love, power rather than cooperation, reputation rather than community, pleasure rather than happiness, pride rather than fulfillment, image rather than sincerity, and material gain rather than personal satisfaction. It desires what I want for myself rather than what the Spirit wants for his creation.

It desires me rather than God.

To live according to the flesh is to live a life turned inward. That's why, when I'm living a primitive life focused only on the selfish desires of my body and brain, I feel like I'm running into a wall. Frustrated and bruised.

When I focus on myself for too long, I find that my world becomes awfully small. I spend less time enjoying my friends and more time wondering what my friends think of me. I spend less time laughing and more time consumed with what's wrong with my life. I spend less time being satisfied with my life and more time shopping for distractions. I spend less time being creative, energetic, and happy and more time trying to fill those holes with cheap imitations that never seem to do the job. When I am focused on the flesh —when I'm dominated by myself — even the quality moments are nothing but happy-meal prizes. They're colorful and fun, but they break easily and usually end up lost.

When I live my life turned inward, I usually end up doing the things of which I am most ashamed. I become consumed by much that is trivial and dangerous.

That's why those who are still under the control of their sinful nature cannot please God. When I let myself be controlled by my flesh — by aggression, irritation, selfishness, lust, pride — I can't please God. I can't please God because I'm not even trying. I am turned inward, focusing my attention toward other things. Things that don't matter. Things of the flesh. Things that eventually die and rot.

I want to please God, but how can I when I'm so totally focused on myself, paying attention only to what I want, considering only myself?

I think I please God when I'm living my life to its fullest. When I'm using my talents as they were meant to be used, when my personality and relationships are full of life and love, when my eyes and ears are turned toward both the beauty and need of the world around me, I feel that I am pleasing to God.

When I am living according to my flesh, I'm turned inward (and usually unhappy). When I am living life according to the spirit, I'm living a life turned outward (and feeling much more fulfilled). When I'm controlled by the Holy Spirit of God, I turn my mind toward things of the Spirit. This doesn't mean that I'm only allowed to think about missions or what Jesus would do. It means that I raise my eyes long enough to realize that there is a world of goodness beyond my small porch of a life. It means that I realize that the world revolves around the sun. And I don't even live on the sun. It means that I let myself be freed from the traps I've fallen into. I get over myself. I shift my focus. I turn my life outward.

If your sinful nature controls your mind there is death. But if the Spirit controls your mind there is life and peace.

Not many people realize that the word that the Bible uses for *spirit* can also be translated "wind" or "breath." It's pretty clear in this sentence that the "spirit" God wants to control my mind is really the Holy Spirit of God. But if I let poetry get lost in theology, I miss the beautiful mind of God.

Living life turned outward is living according to the spirit. According to the wind. According to the breath. Living life according to the wind is freedom. Living life according to the breath is peace. Living according to the Spirit is living life as life. It's the freedom of being released from my own reflection and being set free to soar in a bigger sky. It's looking up and realizing that living focused on myself is living life small, confined, and limited. But I've been set free to focus on something other than myself. I've been set free to focus on things other than what my flesh desires.

I've been set free to turn away from the mirror and enjoy the freedom of a larger world.

I love a good movie as much as the next guy. I even enjoy seeing a movie on opening day. But only after a really good night's sleep.

But a concert is another story. I think most people would agree that it's cool to spend the night on a sidewalk waiting for tickets to a great concert. Camping out to see Dave Matthews, U2, or the Rolling Stones is a respectable adventure. Even if you don't agree with a person's taste in music, you have to admire the dedication of one who craves music over comfort.

This person recognizes that at a concert he will experience his favorite song as it was meant to be heard. Live. Loud. Driven not by a producer but by the passion of a moment. And that immortal moment cannot be duplicated. That song will never again be played exactly the same way as it was for that crowd at that arena. That song is worth sleeping in a bag on the cold, hard ground.

It is this sidewalk-filling mentality that made the Grateful Dead grateful.

I'm not a sports fan, but even I can admit that making a pilgrimage to see your favorite team play on their home field or court must be an exhilarating experience. Movies document a boy's first gaze upon Wrigley Field or the home of the

Fighting Irish as a holy time, a spiritual moment that makes old men cry and bonds fathers and sons for a lifetime.

It must be amazing to see your favorite team do battle on their home field. To see sports heroes who have been immortalized on television and in magazines sweat and compete in living color must be inspiring. The game is a contest that will never be repeated. It will be played this way only once. It will end this way only once. These contests inspire boys to grow strong and eat their vegetables. They inspire college students to paint their bodies and sing songs of unending allegiance. They inspire middle-aged men to buy nachos and drink beer.

I don't know about body painting, but a good tub of nachos is definitely worth a road trip.

Movies, however, are different. Movies play every afternoon, evening, and weekend at the local cineplex. The same movie will play on the same screen for weeks. The same actors will always deliver the same lines in the same way. The same cars will explode, the same lovers will kiss, and the same Anakin will turn into the same Darth every time the projector rolls. It won't change. There will be no surprise interceptions or overtimes or records broken. There will be no encores or reunions. The ring will always be dropped into the fires of Mt. Doom, and Jack Nicholson will never be able to handle the truth. The movie will play the same way every time.

What is it, then, that would possess people to sit in line overnight waiting for opening night tickets to certain cult-favorite movies? Do these fans not know that if they will just wait a week, they can see the same movie on the same screen without having to sleep on a sidewalk with people dressed in hooded capes carrying swords and sabers? If they'll just wait a week, they can save themselves the agony of being kept awake all night by middle-aged computer programmers endlessly debating whether Neo really is the one. If they'll just wait a week, they can buy tickets without ever having to hear, "Please turn off your light saber. I'm trying to get some sleep."

But I shouldn't pass judgment. When the closing chapter of a certain epic movie trilogy released awhile ago, my buddy Greg and I made a road trip to see it with some buddies in North Carolina. The movie was playing at 12:01 a.m. on its opening day. A friend had tickets to a special showing at a theater reputed to have the best sound system east of some significant landmark. I forget which landmark. Probably a mountain or a river or an exceptionally tall building the next town over. Regardless, every screen in this particular theater would be showing the same movie. Each would document Frodo's hike up the mountain and the subsequent salvation of Middle Earth. The exact same story would be repeated in this theater on this screen for weeks to come. But only on this one night could I see it with my buddies in a room full of people dressed as elves.

Watching a movie surrounded by elves? You can't tell me that's not worth a road trip.

Most of our trip to North Carolina was uneventful. For much of the seven hour drive, Greg and I rode in the comfortable silence that surrounds men who know each other well. We drank Dr. Pepper and turned the music up loud. After about four hours, when the Jeep's tank had emptied and Greg's had filled, we stopped at a gas station just short of the

North Carolina border in East Tennessee to take care of our respective fluid problems. We were preparing to get back onto the interstate when I saw a woman standing on the shoulder of the entrance ramp next to an old broken-down sedan.

Her name was Kooter. She spelled it with a "K."

Honestly, I don't usually stop to help people stranded on the side of the road. I guess I probably should. I assume Jesus would. Unfortunately, I don't have nearly as much in common with Jesus as I would like. But this was an exception. Something in the woman's desperate expression forced me to pull the Jeep to the side of the road. It was a good thing I did.

Her car sat tilted with its right front bumper resting on the ground. The corresponding wheel had completely detached from its axle. The amputated wheel lay in the gravel a few feet away. The car looked like it had lost a tooth. With its nose down, the machine appeared humbled, like it was sniffing for a place to bury something. The woman stood with hands on hips, a cigarette perched delicately on her lip. She also looked like she was searching for a place to bury something. But a 1972 Buick requires a pretty big hole.

The woman introduced herself by saying that her name was Kooter. "With a K." The "K" was obviously important, more so than any of the other letters in her name. I knew this because she didn't make an issue of either of the other consonants. Kooter didn't say so, but I could tell that the "K" made her feel like a lady. The difference between Kooter and Cooter is the difference between Kris and Chris. One letter is the difference between a damsel in distress and a dude who can't fix his own car. In rural East Tennessee this is apparently an important distinction.

Kooter's car was in serious trouble. Upon further inspection it became evident that the wheel had not simply come loose from its axle. The axle itself had snapped at the joint, breaking the metal into two pieces. The steel rod was completely fractured. Kooter had been driving happily down the entrance ramp when the entire wheel just popped off.

It was a sad story. Greg kicked the tire. Kicking a car's tire is the mechanical equivalent of a doctor taking a child's temperature. It's a test of wellness. But I don't think this test works after the tire has been separated from the car. The disembodied tire bore witness to the fact that Kooter's car was not well. Greg might as well have been taking the pulse of a severed arm.

But Kooter's eyes shone with hope. She asked, "Do you think you can fix it?"

I didn't think we could. I had foolishly left my spot-welder at home.

But Kooter wasn't discouraged. She was thankful that two nice boys had driven by and been kind enough to stop. Kooter said she was on her way to meet her husband, a long-distance trucker who was due to arrive by bus within the hour. His Greyhound station was at the next exit, only a few miles up the road. We offered her a ride. Kooter gratefully accepted and asked if we'd mind waiting while she got a few important things out of the front seat. I told her to take her time.

A few important things.

Greg and I watched as Kooter reached for a pack of cigarettes resting on the dashboard. She left her purse, wallet, and cell phone sitting in plain view, abandoned on the front seat.

After she slammed the door, I asked Kooter if she had everything she needed, amazed at what she had chosen to leave behind. The question brought her back from a dream. She was obviously rattled by the day's events. "No," she said. "I'm such a dummy. Wait just a second." And she reached back into the car, fumbled around in her purse, and retrieved a green disposable lighter. "Now I'm ready," she announced. And nicotine fix in hand, our motley fellowship made its way to the bus station where Kooter would reunite with her love.

She could come back for her cash, identification, and credit cards later. But the smokes were important.

A lady has to focus on what's important.

And so do I. But sometimes, like Kooter, I get distracted. It's not that Kooter didn't know that a driver's license and Master Card are harder to replace than a pack of Marlboros, but she was flustered. Distracted. It had been a big day. Her car lost a limb. She was reuniting with her husband. Who wouldn't have temporarily lost focus? Who wouldn't have chosen a smoke over a phone call or money for a meal?

I am as easily distracted as Kooter. Sometimes I lose my focus. Sometimes the things that pass through my day erase all my good intentions and fill the space with chaos. It's not that I don't know right from wrong. It's not that I don't believe God is important. It's not that I don't realize my sin separates me from everything good. It's not that I can't understand that the Spirit is life but the flesh is death. It's just that I'm easily distracted. I lose sight of what matters and turn my attention toward what I think will make me happy.

It takes about one second for my ADHD spirituality to jump tracks. One day I feel so close to God that I can practically feel his breath in my ear. And then, as life fades into life, I lose it. My mind fills with garbage and clutter and filth, and I wonder where it all came from. Where it all went. One day I feel so certain. The next, I'm not sure. One day I feel committed and the next, lazy.

And I wonder at what point it all went wrong.

It scares me how easy it is to take my eyes off what's important and walk away. Not because I want to reject Jesus or turn my back on faith and God, but because I so quickly lose sight of what I've known to be good. And when I do forget and turn my attention, I feel like I've left something important behind. Like I'm not quite whole. Not quite complete. Like I've abandoned something I once knew was important in exchange for a cheap green lighter and a pack of cigarettes.

And I have. I've settled for trash when the valuables were sitting in plain view. I have taken my eyes off Jesus, the author and perfecter of my faith. I have wasted my time with things that don't matter. Things that are dangerous. Things that left me less alive. I regret this because I know that the Spirit is life. And even though I only sort of know what that means, I can feel that it's true.

I would rather have life than regret. I'd rather be Spirit-led than self-absorbed. So I pray that God will turn my eyes toward what makes his spirit happy. And I pray that he will cause those things to make my spirit happy too. I pray that he will turn my attention away from the things that are not important so they will no longer hold me back. I pray that he will set me free from myself. Because sometimes I make poor choices. And sometimes I don't like what I see when the reflection stares back at me.

Garden State may be one of my all-time favorite movies. If I knew I was going to be stranded on a deserted island, I would definitely take it along. *Garden State* is a beautiful story about the random journey we all make through life. Natalie Portman plays the cute young girl who is innocent but still mischievous and fun. The kind of girl every guy dreams of. Zach Braff plays Andrew Largeman, who is more than a little odd. But the kind of odd that makes him intriguing.

In one of my favorite scenes, Andrew sits at the breakfast table with his best friend, his best friend's mom, and his best friend's mom's boyfriend, who happens to be dressed as a medieval knight. They sit in the haze of the previous night's party, awkward because the boyfriend and the son went to high school together. And the boyfriend is still dressed as a medieval knight. Eating cereal. Awkward.

To break the strained silence, the mom turns to the cereal-eating boyfriend and says, "It's good, isn't it? I always try to save a couple of the marshmallows to the very end, but I never make it. I always end up with a bunch of the flake things and pink milk. My mind wanders."

Mine too. I get distracted. I wish I could focus on …

The Bible tells us that "since we are surrounded by such a huge crowd of witnesses to the life of faith, [we should] strip off every weight that slows us down, especially the sin that so easily hinders our progress. And let us run with endurance the race that God has set before us. We do this by keeping our eyes on Jesus, on whom our faith depends from start to finish." [2]

Strip the weight. Run with endurance. Fix your eyes. Good advice. It comes just after the author has recounted the stories of a long list of people who took their eyes off the limitations of their circumstance or the guilt of their lifestyle and turned their attention toward a greater goal. They were set free from themselves. They turned away from what wasn't important and saw that a greater race had been marked out for them. They had purpose. They threw off their weighted lives so they could run toward this purpose with endurance. Without distraction. They took their eyes off what didn't matter so they could focus on what did.

As a result, they have been immortalized as some of history's greatest examples of faith. All because they chose to turn away from what wasn't important and focus on what was. They overcame their doubt, fear, guilt, and insecurity by focusing on something greater than themselves.

It's wise advice. A life turned inward is death. But a life focused and controlled by the Spirit is life, peace, and purpose.

I would like to live those wise words. I would really like

to follow the example of their lives. I would like to strip off the weights that slow me down. I would like to get untangled from the sin that is hindering my progress, pulling me back, holding me down, and stealing my focus. It's diverting my attention from things I know are important. A race has been marked for me. I am part of a greater plan. I want to see that plan and run toward it. I don't want to be distracted. I want to run with endurance.

Maybe I should decide what's important and try to leave everything else behind.

Kooter chose a lighter and a wad of cigs over her wallet and cell phone. But I can do better. Stephen can't seem to see that there is a big, big world outside his own reflection. But I can lift my gaze.

I can take my eyes off what isn't important. I can stop jealously focusing on the success of my friends and should-be friends. I can release my own insecurity about myself and what will happen tomorrow and the day after that. I can turn away from the flashing images of my computer screen. I can turn my attention from the flesh and onto the Spirit. I can strip off all the weights that have slowed me down, and I can run with endurance the race that has been set before me.

I will only run the race well when I keep my eyes on Jesus. If the selfish sinful nature controls my mind, there is only death. But when I turn my attention toward things of the Spirit, I find life and peace.

Being controlled by the Spirit is all about focusing on what's important and leaving everything else behind.

Kooter, if you're out there, don't forget your wallet.

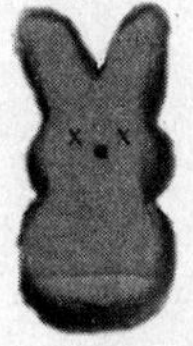

Me again.

You know what I'm doing.

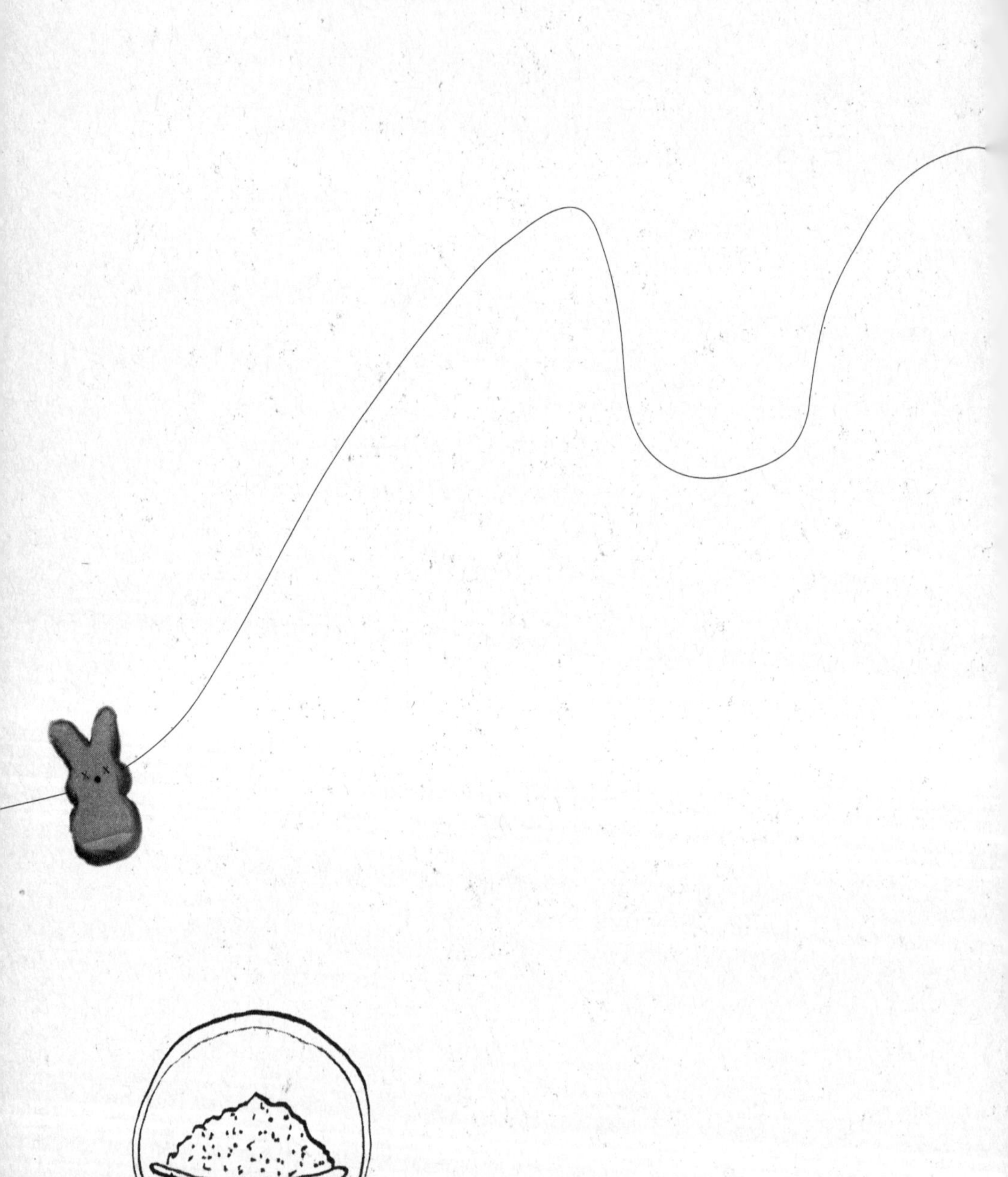

Sand and Balloons

Most people do regular stuff on the weekends. They see a movie, hang out with friends, go to a concert, or sit at home doing nothing. My friends and I are no different. We like the regular stuff. But when something different comes along, we're definitely in for an adventure. Movies are great and parties are fun, but when somebody says they know where we might be able to find a herd of sleeping cows that need pushing over, we're there.

A couple of springs ago, the fair came to town. Nobody can resist a county fair, so my friends and I went. The smell of funnel cakes enticed us. We were lured by grilled corn on the cob and the promise of giant stuffed cartoon character prizes. In the parking field, cars were bathed in the glow of blinking lights as families paid for the screams of delighted (and sometimes terrified) kids.

When we got to the fair, my friend Scott immediately wanted to ride the Tilt-a-Whirl. What the devil was thinking when he invented the Tilt-a-Whirl, I'll never know. If you haven't seen it, the Tilt-a-Whirl is an evil contraption that attempts to spin riders around until their world is a dizzy wreck. Who really wants to pay four dollars just to throw up on someone? I don't. But that's the beauty of America. If you want to be entertained by regurgitating on a stranger, you have that freedom.

But the rides weren't the reason we went to the fair. That was just bonus. The real reason we went was that I had heard about a hypnotist there who did a show every night at nine. You can see a movie anytime. But it's not every day you get to see a real, live hypnotist. It doesn't take much imagination to know that watching some guy in a shiny suit hypnotize folks at the county fair is totally worth the price of admission. When we learned that his stage was located directly next to Walter the High Diving Pig, we knew we were in for an evening of quality entertainment.

By the time we found the hypnotist's stage it was about twenty minutes until the show started, so we took our seats on the metal bleachers and waited. We people watched to pass the time. I hope you have come to the place in your life where you fully realize how fascinating people watching can be. When done correctly, people watching is sport and entertainment all rolled into one. It must be understood that when you people watch, you don't just sit and watch people. That's amateur. We experts (and by "experts" I mean "people with way too much time on their hands") play actual people watching games and keep score.

As a warm-up my friends and I played a few rounds of "Spot the Mullet." (My apologies if you have a mullet of your own.) After this we proceeded to a game of "Do You Think

They're Related?" and a round or two of "Man or Woman?" It was amazing how ripe a playing field the fair proved to be for our sport. Just before the hypnotist took the stage, we even invented a new game just for the occasion. We called it "Who Has Fewer Teeth Than Me?" Big hit. Lots of winners.

Then the show started and our new hypnotist friend walked out onto an elevated stage that was set with a line of about twenty folding chairs. The man looked to be in his mid-forties, black suit, big smile, very TBN. He sauntered onto the stage and started his demonstration by explaining exactly what hypnotism is.

Apparently, it is not as magical as we'd like it to be. It's not like what we see in old James Bond movies or corny television shows. Hypnotized people do not kill on command or awake to find their memories erased and three years of their lives missing. Hypnotism, he explained, is actually a state of deep relaxation where the mind is open to suggestion. But it's only suggestion. He told us that when hypnotized, a person won't do anything he doesn't want to do or anything she finds morally objectionable.

So, after his opening speech, the hypnotist took the entire audience through an exercise that was supposed to determine which of us might be potential subjects. We were instructed to close our eyes, breathe deeply, and retreat to our "happy place." He then told us all to stretch our arms out completely in front of our bodies and open our hands.

"Try to imagine that you can see through your eyelids," he said. "Look at your hands. Open them. Close them. Look through your eyelids and see their every movement. Can you see your hands?"

Two hundred people nodded their heads obediently.

One kid was peeking. Cheater.

The rest of us were taken in by his spell. We were in our happy places. We could see our hands. This was great. Then he said, "I'm placing a beautiful bouquet of balloons in your right hand. There are twelve of them and they are lighter than air. Red balloons. Can you see them?"

We nodded yes.

"The balloons dance and play in the breeze. They float and pull in your hand. Gently tugging up, up, up. Hold on to them. Don't let them go. Can you feel the balloons?"

We could feel them.

"Now, with your left hand, reach out and take the bucket that I'm handing you. It's a plastic bucket like the kind you'd give a child to take to the beach. Green. Hold the handle of the bucket in your left hand. Do you have the bucket?"

Yes.

"Now, hold on tightly. I'm putting one shovel-full of sand in your bucket. I know it's heavy, but try to keep holding your arm out straight."

We tried, but it was heavy.

"I'm putting one more shovel of sand in your bucket. And even though you're strong, your left shoulder is tired and you can feel the bucket sinking down, down, down. But your right hand is light and free. You can feel the balloons pulling up, up, up. It's all you can do to keep them from flying away. But your left arm feels very heavy. I'm putting another large scoop of sand in the bucket. You don't think you can hold it any longer. It's so heavy. The balloons are so light. Feel the bucket sink down! Feel the balloons pull up! Now … slowly open your eyes."

We did. About two-thirds of us were sitting with our right arm high over our head and our left arm pointing toward the ground. We looked like a bunch of second-graders learning to clap. I was one of them. My left arm was heavy and tired, my right arm straight up in the air. I wished I had remembered to wear deodorant.

He then told us that if our hands were spread apart more than a couple of feet, we were prime candidates for hypnotism. We were able to visualize. We were able to let go. "If you are willing to let go even further," he said, "come on up to the stage and take a seat. Let's see how far we can take this."

It took less than a minute for all twenty chairs to fill. The hypnotist started his act by telling his victims (or volunteers or suckers or whatever you want to call them) to focus on a point far off in space and relax.

"Imagine that you're the only person on the planet," he said. "Focus on a far-off point and breathe deeply. Relax your feet. Relax your legs. Inhale and let yourself go. Feel the air moving through you. Exhale and feel the tension melting away. Relax your chest. Relax your neck …"

They looked so comfortable.

"Now," he said, "your body feels like it's melting. Your head feels heavy. Your neck is so relaxed that it can't hold your head up. Let your head fall. Breathe. Feel your eyes slowly become heavy and close. The night is warm and your muscles just want to rest. Let go. Close your eyes and let go."

I have never seen anything like it. Each of the twenty people on stage sat sleepy and slumped over in their chairs like fat Uncle Ed after Thanksgiving dinner. The hypnotist then told them to focus on their "happy place," the one perfect place on earth where they would feel content and serene. Not to pass judgment, but from the looks of this crowd, most of their happy places involved four-wheelers, camouflage, and bottled deer urine. Not that there's anything wrong with that. I like deer urine as much as the next guy. I'm just not sure that there's a supply of animal pee in my happy place.

The hypnotist kept taking the group deeper and deeper, making them more and more relaxed until each person on stage sat in a chair wilted like a plate of wet spaghetti. These twenty people were so relaxed, so completely uninhibited, so incredibly passed out that they were lying all over each other like a Daytona Beach spring break after-party.

Then the hypnotist said to us in the audience, "Now that I have 'em, look at what I can do with 'em!"

He started by convincing the group it was hot outside. Of course, this was August in Tennessee, so it really was hot outside. Not too much of a stretch. But he had these people convinced that it was not only hot, it was Mojave Desert hot. Frying pan pavement hot. Paris Hilton hot. And you could tell they were feeling it. They were burning up. They fanned and sweated. It wasn't until a lady tried to find relief by taking off her shirt that the hypnotist snapped his fingers and sent them back to their happy places. A few of us were disappointed.

Then he took his deception the other direction and told his subjects how cold it was outside. "When I snap my fingers," he said, "it will no longer be hot. At my command, it will only be thirty degrees outside." Snap.

Instantly everyone on stage began to shiver and shake.

"When I snap my fingers this time, it will only be eight degrees outside. And don't forget that you're only wearing shorts and a T-shirt." Snap.

They went crazy. The people on stage sat hugging themselves, rubbing their arms for warmth, and blowing hot breath into cupped hands. You could tell that they really were freezing. Incredible.

"This time when I snap my fingers, it will be ten degrees below zero, and the only way you'll be able to stay warm is to share body heat with the person next to you." Snap.

At this point, the hypnotized people could have been faking it, but I don't think so. Down on the end of the row there was an eighteen-year-old guy sitting next to a forty-something-year-old lady. He was a normal looking eighteen-year-old guy, but she was frightening. At some point in this woman's life, a doctor had clearly told her to eat a balanced meal, and she went out and had a cup of coffee, a pack of cigarettes, and some chewing gum. Even from my seat I could sense that this woman actually smelled mean. Somebody desperately needed to inform her that tobacco is not generally considered a vegetable. I know that's harsh, but sometimes the truth hurts.

And the only place this innocent guy had to go for warmth was into her lap. So he went. He went as if his life depended on it. He climbed her like a tree.

And then the games began.

In the middle of this artic adventure, the hypnotist told the group that when he snapped his fingers every person on stage was going to wake up, open their eyes, and know exactly where they were. And it was going to be funny because these people were all over each other and weren't going to know how they got there. Sure enough, when the hypnotist snapped his fingers, the woman on the end opened her eyes to find this innocent young thing cuddled up in her lap.

And she came completely unglued. In one fluid movement, Zena jumped up from the chair, tossed the kid on the floor, and channeled the spirit of Jerry Springer. From my seat on the bleachers, I could see nothing but fists and fur. All the guy could do was roll into a ball as he got the funnel cake beaten out of him. When the hypnotist saw what was happening, he quietly strolled across the stage, touched the top of Zena's head, snapped his fingers, and boom — she fell fast asleep in a puddle on the floor. Wet spaghetti.

Incredible.

For the next trick he had one of the hypnotized guys lie stretched out between three chairs. The guy's head rested on one chair and his feet rested on another. The third supported his butt. Then the hypnotist told this guy to imagine that he was as stiff as a board. Every cell in his body had turned to concrete. All of his joints had fused and his body was a solid slab. Unbreakable. Unbendable.

Once the hypnotist was convinced that the man had become a human sidewalk, he brought a woman up from the audience and asked her to stand on his stomach. Stand on his stomach. Right on his belly button. She did. And just as the lady was getting her balance, the hypnotist pulled the chair out from under the guy's butt. He was suspended two feet above the ground supported only by his head and feet with a full grown woman standing on his stomach. I saw it with my own eyes. Maybe this guy was superhuman, but I don't think so. From what I could tell, he was just a regular guy. You may have abs of steel, but this guy didn't. He had an ab of jelly doughnut and a full-grown woman standing right on top of it.

Incredible. You can't fake that.

I was hooked.

Of course, my friends and I went back the next week. I was determined to be one of the suckers on stage. Sitting on the same bleachers, in front of the same stage, next to the same high-diving pig, we waited as the hypnotist went through his whole pail of sand, handful of balloons thing. Like Edward Scissorarms, I was into it. He called for volunteers and I hopped up on stage, the first one there. Just like the week before, he had us breathe in through our noses and out through our mouths, and our eyes got heavy, and he directed us to go to our happy places.

I was picturing my happy place in my mind and trying

to keep it G-rated, but for some reason Halle Berry always shows up in my happy place. Regardless, I was sitting on stage and I was relaxed and I was feeling fine, but I was also deciding how far I was going to take this thing. I mean, how much should I trust this random guy to dig around in my brain? I know he said I wouldn't do anything I didn't want to do, but I've got some files up there that I don't really want anybody double clicking on. And if somebody is going to rewrite my hard drive, I'm not sure I want it to be a side-show hypnotist who spends his life at state fairs eating funnel cakes and smoking out back with the Bearded Lady and Walter the High Diving Pig. I've got enough problems without this guy pimpin' my ride. I can't afford to wake up in the morning thinking I'm the Queen of England.

So as much as I wanted to be in, there was still a little doubt. But I was relaxed, I was trying to be wet spaghetti, and I could hear everything the hypnotist was saying. He told us how heavy our eyes were. He relaxed every part of our body. And then the first gag was going to be that he would have us envision somebody pinching our eyes shut. He told us that when he counted to three, we were going to try to open our eyes but wouldn't be able to. And it would be funny because everybody would be stretching their faces trying to open their eyes only to find that they couldn't. I could see how this was going to be comical, but in my mind I was thinking, *You have got to be kidding. I can open my eyes anytime I want to.*

And I was right.

He counted, "One … two … three… open!" And just as I

thought, *Thanks Dr. Phil, I think I will!* I opened my eyes … and I was naked.

Just kidding. I wasn't naked. That would be weird. And not just regular weird. Michael Jackson weird. I wasn't naked. I was fine. I was no different than I had been thirty minutes before. But maybe that was the point. I wasn't naked. I hadn't done anything stupid. I was just sitting on a stage at the fair. When I went up on stage I wanted the hypnotist to make me do the Boot Scootin' Boogie with underwear on my head. But in the end I just sat in my seat watching everybody look like idiots as they tried unsuccessfully to open their own eyes.

The whole reason I went to the show is because I wanted to lose control. I wanted to trust the hypnotist and let go, but I ended up sitting on a stage looking at a bunch of people looking at me wondering why my eyes weren't glued shut. I continued to wonder the same thing all the way to my seat.

I talked with the hypnotist after the show. I wanted to know why it didn't work. He told me that in the end it all came down to me deciding if I was in or out. If I wasn't completely in, if I didn't completely let go, it would not work. I had to decide if I could believe this was real and trust a man I didn't know and let myself be sucked in. If I could, great. If not, nothing was going to happen. Success depended on my ability to willingly and completely surrender.

When it comes to this Jesus thing, lots of people I know are still deciding, "Am I in, or am I out?" How much do I believe? How much do I trust? Can I really let go? How far am I willing to take this thing before I give up and go back to my seat? Can I trust this guy I barely know to have total control of me, or am I going to end up looking like an idiot?

They are good questions.

I want to let go. I want to give him complete control. I do. But I'm afraid. I know that I was created for a purpose and I've been told that God has a plan for my life. But I can't see it. So I doubt. And sometimes I suspect I miss a great show all because I'm not willing to let go.

Of course, a relationship with Jesus is not a circus trick or mind control. Letting go doesn't require me to shut down my brain, abandon all logic, and refuse to ask questions or doubt or struggle. A God who would require that would be a terribly insecure God. A follower who bought into such a relationship would be in danger of drinking tainted Kool-Aid.

Letting go means I am willing to give Jesus access to my mind, heart, and decisions. It means I'm willing to walk with him through the process. Sometimes I do that pretty well. Other times, not so much. But at the end of the day it's a choice. My choice.

God doesn't force anything on me.

It seems like I've run into many people over the past few years who really enjoy playing with spirituality. They're not exactly "in," but they're "around." They like the mental game that the idea of God presents. They treat God and religion and faith like a hobby. A philosophy or thought they like chewing on. A series of obscure, old, or trendy books they like to say they have read. This irritates me. This irritates me because it seems that these people are seeking God, but they're not. They're really just seeking some way to prove to themselves or the people around them that they are smart or different or deep.

But they're not in.

Seeking God is not asking questions just for the sake of asking questions. Seeking God is not being antagonistic just to prove that you're a thinker who doubts sometimes or is willing to say what nobody else is saying. Seeking is making an effort to move in a direction that will help you make a decision about who God might want you to be or what he might want you to do. It's actually moving in a direction.

My friends and I have a saying that we use when we're irritated with people who refuse to make difficult decisions. We say, "Get in or get out. Just get." (Some people modify this saying to include either pots or ladders, but I'm sure you get the idea.)

Maybe when Jesus told us to be either hot or cold, that was his way of telling us to decide how in we are. Get in or get out. Just get.

To be honest, when I was on stage at the fair, there was a moment when I said to myself, "Everybody's watching. Maybe I can fake it. They'll never know the difference. I could do whatever this guy tells me to do and put on a good show. Nobody has to know." And I was capable of that. I could have played the game. I could have put on a brilliant performance. I could have faked it. Nobody would have known.

Except me.

I think I'm beginning to understand that there's a significant difference between living a good moral life and having an actual relationship with Jesus. There are lots of churchy people out there who can quote Bible verses and sing songs and

act the part well. These are generally good moral people. But honestly, I wonder how many of them are faking it. I wonder if they're really as spiritual as they seem. I wonder how many of them are actually experiencing God and how many of them are putting on a brilliant performance.

At the same time, I sometimes wonder the same thing about myself. How often do I close my eyes during someone else's prayer over a meal because I too am thankful, and how often am I faking it? How often do I tell my friend that I'll pray for him and then actually pray for him, and how often do I fake it? How often do I act spiritual and certain because that's what's expected of me, and how often do I fake it?

I have a friend named Ryan who has more potential than most people on the planet. During high school he was pretty committed to being a follower of Jesus. But at some point he changed his mind. Ryan has a lot of problems. One of his most significant problems is that he is an addict. Ryan knows that he's an addict. But getting help scares him.

Like most addicts, Ryan will do almost anything to convince the people around him that he doesn't have a problem. I know Ryan lies to his dad. I'm pretty sure Ryan lies to me. And I'm certain Ryan lies to himself. When he talks I can't decide if he's trying to convince the world that he's okay or if he's trying to convince himself that he's okay. Either way, he's not okay.

About a month ago Ryan hit the bottom and broke. He caused a car accident and received his second DUI in a year. Ryan called to say that he'd had enough. I don't know if he was just saying this because he knew it was what I wanted to hear, but I believed Ryan when he told me, "Bryan, I just can't do this anymore. I've tried to do everything for myself for so long. And it's not working. There has to be something better out there."

He wasn't faking it anymore.

So we started talking about treatment. I gave my friend the names, numbers, and web addresses of half a dozen centers that could help him get straightened out. I was hopeful. But he was scarred. He couldn't imagine what life would be like after treatment. He couldn't see that the other side would be any better than what he's living now. He couldn't imagine a change. So he didn't go.

In the meantime, Ryan has continued to get drunk and high. Even after his beautiful confession, he has continued to medicate his life away. A week ago Ryan's dad found him bombed out of his mind on prescription painkillers. Ryan denied that anything was wrong. He denied that he was high. He denied that that there was a problem. And that's the problem. He's faking it again.

If Ryan would just sit down for twelve minutes and have a hard, honest conversation with himself, I really think he might be okay. But for him to do that, he is going to have to be honest with himself about himself. No more denial. And that honesty is going to result in some difficult decisions. He is going to have to let go.

In one of the Psalms, King David wrote, "Surely you desire truth in the inner parts; you teach me wisdom in the inmost place." Another translation renders this sentence: "You desire honesty from the heart, so you can teach me to be wise in my inmost being." [1]

Maybe true wisdom comes from being honest with yourself about yourself.

David wrote these words during his own personal meltdown. He had just been caught in an affair with a married woman. In an effort to cover up his affair, he had the woman's husband killed. The woman then gave birth to David's illegitimate child, who later died. In the midst of this ancient soap opera, a wise friend forced David to look honestly at himself.

In his catharsis David cried, "Have mercy on me, O God, because of your unfailing love. Because of your great compassion, blot out the stain of my sins. Wash me clean from my guilt. Purify me from my sin. For I recognize my shameful deeds — they haunt me day and night. Against you, and you alone, have I sinned; I have done what is evil in your sight. You will be proved right in what you say, and your judgment against me is just. For I was born a sinner — yes, from the moment my mother conceived me. But you desire honesty from the heart, so you can teach me to be wise in my inmost being. Purify me from my sins, and I will be clean; wash me and I will be whiter than snow." [2]

I sometimes have a hard time letting go and giving in because I know what I'm hiding. I have a hard time being honest with myself (or God or anyone else) about myself because I know what lives in the dark corners of my soul. I

recognize my shameful deeds. They haunt me day and night.

I'm just terrified that if I let go, someone will expose me as a fraud and send me away.

Faking it is easier. Letting go requires an honesty and vulnerability that seriously frightens me. That's why I avoid prayer. That's why I'm timid at church and in worship. That's why my conversations are shallow and my Bible remains dusty. Letting go requires honesty. And honesty is terrifying because when I am honest with myself about myself (or with God about myself, or with anyone else about myself), then I am sometimes confronted with difficult realizations about myself. And since I don't want to be confronted with that, I fake it.

Maybe true wisdom comes from being honest with yourself about yourself.

But with God there is no faking it. The wisdom of God is full of living power. It is sharper than the sharpest knife, cutting deep into our innermost thoughts and desires. It exposes us for what we really are. Nothing in all creation can hide from him. Everything is naked and exposed before his eyes. This is the God to whom we must explain all that we have done. [3]

There are no secrets. There is no faking it. God knows everything. Like every kid in the United States education system, I encountered that super-human elementary school teacher who told us that she could see everything we did even while she was writing on the chalk board. Even when her back was turned to the class she knew who was whispering, who was writing and/or passing notes, who was not paying attention, and who was preparing to throw pencil erasers at the girls across the room. She said that she had eyes in the back of her head. I often wondered if this made it difficult for her to brush her hair. But regardless of their freakish optical powers, I knew with tried certainty that my teachers were aware of my every move. I was passionate, even at a young age, that the Constitution needed an amendment prohibiting such an invasion of my privacy. I had no secrets.

Unfortunately, the evidence of scripture is that God has also penetrated my mind and soul with his all-seeing gaze. He has eyes in the back of my head. I have been cut open. Gutted like a fish. Exposed for what I am. I have no secrets.

God knows everything. And that scares me to death.

But while the thought that God knows everything may seem like horrifyingly bad news, it also has its good side. Yes, God knows my darkest secrets. Yes, he has witnessed my most shameful deeds. Yes, he has heard my petty conversations, seen my private moments, and had access to my secret thoughts. Yes, I have been cut open and exposed for what I really am. But that is why we have a great High Priest who has gone to heaven, Jesus the Son of God. So I will take the advice of scripture and cling to him and never stop trusting him. I don't have to be afraid because this High Priest of mine understands my weaknesses. He faced all of the same temptations I do, yet he did not sin. So I will come boldly to the throne of my gracious God. There I will receive his mercy, and I will find grace to help me when I need it.

The good news is that God has experienced life as one of us. He not only knows us completely, he understands us completely.

I can trust God for the same reason that I'm often afraid of him. Because he knows me for what I am. He knows my secrets and hasn't gone screaming into the night. I trust him not only because he knows me for what I am, but because he knows me as I am. God wrapped himself in skin and walked the earth with us so that I could know that he understands. He is not God sequestered in heaven. He is Jesus among his people. He gets it.

I wouldn't trust a doctor who is always sick. I wouldn't trust a math teacher who hasn't mastered long division. I can't trust a dentist with no teeth or a waitress who is afraid to eat the soup of the day. But I can trust a God who understands my weakness because he has experienced the same temptations I have. I can respect him because he did so without making the same mistakes I have. And I can approach him boldly to ask for his mercy when I need it because I know he gets me. His knowledge of me is the reason he has compassion for me. And so I feel no fear in his love.

I'll never feel connected with God as long as I'm hiding behind my shame, guilt, or secrecy. How could I? Secrets don't breed trust. Love doesn't grow in fear. It's only in my moments of unrestrained honesty that I can truly feel the mercy, grace, and love of God. It's only when I'm unguarded that that I find an authentic relationship. It's only when I expose the scariest parts of myself that I feel the true acceptance of God.

But you desire honesty from the heart, so you can teach me to be wise in my inmost being.

Wisdom says that there's really no point in faking it. Any of it. With anybody. In the end, honesty is my only option.

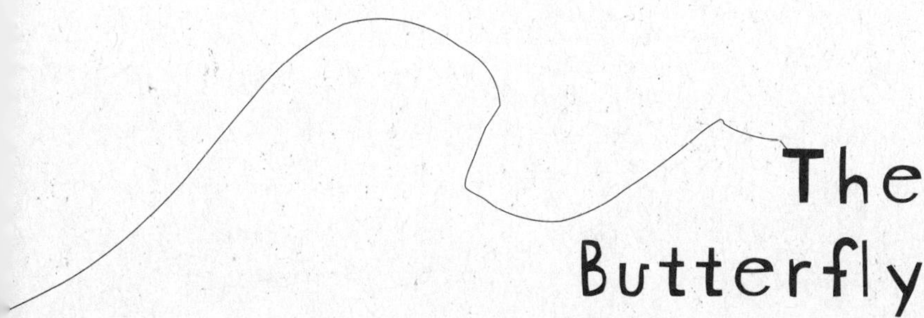

The Butterfly

I like butterflies as much as the next guy. Unless they're thirteen years old. And naked.

I was spending the weekend in a house full of middle-schoolers. As Neverland as that may sound, I probably find myself in this situation more than the average person. A youth minister friend of mine had asked me to come and lead an in-home Bible study that would be a part of a discipleship weekend for his youth group. He wanted me to teach the eighth graders. I happily agreed.

I may be in a distinct minority, but I like eighth graders. Maybe it's because I get identified as an adult when I'm with middle-school students. Maybe I have a Willy Wonka-esque obsession with small people. But mostly I think I like eighth-grade people because I love the energy, creativity, and life that you find when you hang out with teenagers. And middle-schoolers have an abundance of energy, creativity, and life.

Especially the butterfly.

My group of about twelve eighth graders were incredible people. And by incredible, I mean energetic. And by energetic, I mean out of control. Totally out of control. During our first hour together, four of the twelve kids (in case your calculator is broken, that's approximately one third) informed me that they needed to be reminded to take their ADHD medication at least twice daily. Another two told me that while they also took medication for their hyperactivity during the school week, the weekends were free time. Apparently on the weekends even sanity takes a vacation. Fantastic.

I was concerned at first that such a high percentage (about half) of the people I would be confined to a house with for the next forty-eight hours required supplementary chemicals to keep their minds and bodies under control. It sounded like a movie plot waiting to be written. And our movie would definitely star either the industrious (if not slightly irritating) kid from *Home Alone* or Sponge Bob Square Pants himself. Or maybe the Tazmanian Devil. With an energy drink.

At least these kids were aware that they needed to take medication. The magic pills these students take are intended to give hyperactive people the super-human ability to control their impulses while sitting still and focusing on a single task. It's like anti-coffee. I'm not ADHD, but if I ever find a pill that helps me control my impulses while focusing my mind on whatever I'm supposed to be doing, I'm taking it. Twice daily. With milk.

It was completely understandable that these four pubescent angels would ask for a reminder to take their pills. If you have to take medication to help you pay attention, it only stands to reason that you might occasionally forget to take your medicine in the first place. Unfortunately, three of the four had forgotten to bring the medicine I was supposed to remind them to take. One of them was the butterfly.

I now had five kids who needed drugs to control themselves but didn't have the drugs they needed to control themselves. We were all feeling a bit out of control. As a result of this pharmaceutical fiasco, my group of eighth graders had the attention span of a roomful of crack addicts at Starbucks. They couldn't count to three without being distracted. I even saw one kid who went to pick his nose, and halfway there he forgot what he was doing and poked himself in the eye. It was going to be a fun weekend.

Our first full day together went fine, but we did experience a slight bump during the morning Bible study. I made the mistake of telling the group that we could do our first lesson on the back porch of the house we had invaded for the weekend. The back porch. Outside. Next to the basketball goal. And the dog. And a neighbor mowing his lawn. We went to the back porch where there were only about a thousand distractions for my hyper-aware Padawan learners. I'm a genius.

I attempted to solve our sensory overload dilemma by running the hyperactivity out of them. Our lesson was supposed to be about Joshua fighting the battle of Jericho. In the story, God tells Joshua that he will crumble the walls surrounding the impenetrable city of Jericho if Joshua will march his relatively small army around the city once a day for six days. It was to be the first Million Man March. Only not for peace and reconciliation. This march was for war and destruction. Apparently they did not yet have a dream. On the seventh day the army was to walk around the city seven times blowing horns, breaking pots, and generally disturbing the peace. When they did, God crumbled the walls of the city and the Israelites reigned victorious.

So instead of simply telling the story, asking thought provoking questions, and leading fun activities that would help these students encounter God through his word, I made them run. Literally run. Around the house. Seven times. During the first lap, my little cherubs raced around the enormous multi-acre yard as if it were a qualifying round for the Olympics. At the end of this lap, each kid collapsed exhausted on the porch. Poor babies. As they lay there helpless and sweating, I gave them a single nugget of truth and said, "Now, take another lap." And they ran again. Then more truth. And more running. And more truth. And another lap. Then a profound thought. And another jog around the house. A quick question. And another lap. One last reflection. And a final sprint.

By the time they learned why Joshua fought the battle of Jericho by walking around the city seven times, the kids had worn a path around the house. Their posture indicated that each probably had an alien gnawing its way out of their side. Everybody lay exhausted and panting for breath. We didn't finish until every kid completed every lap. There was no child left behind. This was education at its finest.

That night I was certain that every drop of excess energy had been squeezed from their bodies and brains. I was wrong.

The guys had been assigned a communal sleeping area in a playroom on the second floor of our house. I (gratefully) had my own private room just down the hall. Before going to bed in the small hours of the morning, I told the guys that they didn't have to go to sleep, but that I would appreciate it if they would at least stay quiet. I didn't want them to disturb the nice people who had been brave enough to allow this herd of rowdiness into their home. An hour later it became necessary for me to calmly ask the guys to please not talk so loudly and to stop jumping on the furniture. Forty-five minutes after that I kept my voice reasonably steady as I informed them that human bowling is not appropriate when God himself is trying to sleep. It was about twenty minutes later that I almost lost my composure entirely when I thought I smelled something burning. It was time for the tribe to go to bed.

And then the butterfly was born.

I thought that the boys had finally gone to sleep when I heard the unmistakable snort of suppressed giggling in the playroom. Note to self: When boys are loud in the middle of the night, it's irritating. When boys are obviously making an effort to suppress their loudness in the middle of the night, Armageddon may be upon us.

So I crept out of my room quietly hoping to catch the guys at whatever they were up to. I rounded the corner of the playroom just in time to see one small boy, seventy innocent pounds of flesh and hair, writhing around on the floor in his sleeping bag surrounded by a delighted audience of his peers. As the boy slithered out of the hole at the head of his sleeping bag, I realized he was narrating a Discovery Channel special.

"Then the caterpillar emerges from the cocoon victorious," he said.

As he said this, the victorious caterpillar freed himself from his down-filled G.I. Joe cocoon and stood, allowing the sleeping bag to puddle around his feet. His small body stood triumphantly, hands on hips, wearing only boxer shorts and a smile.

"It emerges from the cocoon victorious and becomes a butterfly," he continued.

At the word *butterfly*, the boy abruptly snatched his own underwear down around his feet, stepped out of the shorts, and began to dance and fly around the room, jumping naked from one piece of furniture to the next.

"... and becomes a butterfly, which flies away to freedom."

The butterfly was born. And like all wild creatures, he was born naked and unmedicated.

As the naked butterfly flew away from me at four o'clock that morning, showing me his backside, I was reminded of the children's classic bedtime story *Goodnight Moon*. And I laughed.

You'd think that a butterfly flitting around a room without his protective cocoon would be at least mildly embarrassed once he realized that an adult (who is, at this point, still a relative stranger) stands witnessing his metamorphosis and subsequent victory flight. This butterfly was not afraid.

I told him to put his worm away. It was time to go to bed.

Somewhere in his adolescent heart, the butterfly knew he was made for more than G.I. Joe sleeping bags and eighth-grade algebra. He knew that he was made to fly. It was an instinct born inside him. Early in his life, a fairy tale had planted the seed that even ugly ducklings grow into beautiful swans. Comic books taught him that regular kids turn into Spiderman and swing around the city on snot they shoot out of their wrists. A biology lesson taught the butterfly that even squishy green caterpillars emerge from cocoons victorious and ready for flight. The same media that taught him white men can't jump also brought him cheesy R&B songs that helped him believe he could fly. He believed he could touch the sky. He dreamed about it every night and day.

Eternity had been planted in his heart.

In the book of Ecclesiastes, Solomon (who was reputed to be the wisest man who ever lived) said that God "has planted eternity in the human heart, but even so, people cannot see the whole scope of [his] work from beginning to end." [1] Apparently one of the gifts God has given us is the ability to look beyond ourselves and see that there's more to our lives that what we're experiencing. We are creatures who were made to fly but are trapped on earth. We are fish without wings. We hunger for a future that seems just out of reach.

We want to fly. But instead of flying we take our medicine and control our impulses and focus on whatever we're supposed to be doing. Twice daily. With milk.

These days I feel restless in my life. Not exactly tired or burnt out, but restless. Maybe a little bored. There's even a hint of wondering if this is really all there is. The irony is that "this" really isn't all that bad. I have a job that I know how to do, so I do it. I have a network of relationships that I enjoy, so I maintain them. I have built a lifestyle that makes me comfortable, so I check my email, update my online movie queue, fill my Jeep with gas, download music, and do the hundreds of other things that have come to define who I am. It's all very good, but it's also very predictable.

And so I feel restless. Bored. Like there's got to be something more. Something more to my job. Something more to my relationships. Something more to my talents. Something more to my day. Something more. I want to shed the routine and fly.

Maybe my problem is that the grass is always greener on the other side. Or maybe it's that I'm tired of grass and am ready to move to the beach and swim. I'm restless, and I don't know why. I feel like something is holding me back. Like something is broken. And I wonder if it's not at least partially God's fault.

After all, he is the one who planted eternity in my heart.

I have the ability to see beyond the moment. I can look forward to and anticipate the future. And that makes me restless. I feel an unexplainable sense that something greater is on its way. Eternity has not only been planted in my heart, it has taken root and is taking over. The problem is that while I itch for some mysterious future and the possibility it promises, I can't see the scope of what God is doing from beginning to end. Today is all I know for sure. I'm anxious for tomorrow, but that doesn't mean I'm ready for it.

In the classic movie *Indiana Jones and the Last Crusade*, Indiana Jones and his father are on a mission to recover the Holy Grail, the cup of Christ. Indiana's father has spent his life compiling a diary that contains directions to the Grail's resting place. Before the Grail diary is stolen by the Nazis, Indiana tears out several important pages and entrusts them to his friend, a museum curator named Marcus Brody. When the Nazi bad guys examine the diary and find the pages missing, they quickly deduce that Brody has them. One of the bad guys confidently says, "He (that would be Brody) sticks out like a sore thumb. We'll find him."

Indiana bluffs. "Like hell you will. He has a two-day head start on you, which is more than he needs. Brody's got friends in every town and village from here to the Sudan. He speaks a dozen languages, knows every local custom. He'll blend in. Disappear. You'll never see him again. With any luck he's got the Grail already."

But it was a lie. Brody is a virtual idiot. He is definitely not up for the challenge. Indiana's father later asks him why he's worried about Brody and the diary pages. Confused, he says, "You said that he had two days head start. That he would blend in. Disappear."

Indiana replies, "Are you kidding? I made that up. You know Marcus. He got lost once in his own museum."

And that's how I feel. Like an idiot who gets lost in his own museum. I want to be trusted with something larger than myself and believe that I'm up for the task. I want to break free from my medicated life. But I wonder how responsible I really am with what I already have. I question how able I am to do anything truly important. How talented. How competent. How driven. In one of his parables didn't Jesus say that "to those who use well what they've been given, even more will be given, and they will have an abundance. But from those who are unfaithful, even what they have will be taken away"? [2]

I'm trying my best, but sometimes I feel lost in my own

life. Desperate to fly. But with nowhere to go. Eternity is planted in my heart, but the rest of me is trapped in time.

The summer after my sophomore year of college, I spent three months in Poland as a missionary. When I got home, a buddy of mine asked, "what'd ya do this summer?"

I told him, "I went to Poland."

He said, "Poland? What's in Poland ... poles?"

That's right, Einstein. We get video games from Japan, oil from Iraq, and poles from Poland.

And we make jokes about them?

My friend Eric and I went to Poland to teach English as a means of telling the Polish people about Jesus. Unfortunately, there was one major flaw in this plan. Between Polish and English, we knew only one of the languages. And it wasn't Polish. English I feel relatively confident with. I took it for four years in high school and eight years before that. I know at least most of the words. And to be honest, I don't know why our educational system makes us take English every year of our academic career. English is the only thing other than breathing and going to the bathroom that we actually practice every day without someone telling us to. You'd think that would be enough.

During our first weeks in Poland, Eric and I quickly learned that teaching people English as a second language is extremely difficult when you don't know their first language. It's a bit like Stevie Wonder driving himself to Disneyland. He may know where he wants to go, but his chances of getting there are slim at best. So Eric and I became the stereotypical Americans that countless comedians make fun of for speaking loud and slow to non-English speakers, as if these techniques will actually help them understand our language. We shouted at our students as if they were sitting across a football field from us, slowly overprouncing every letter and sound.

"T H I S I S A B O O K. A B O O K."

(I would never presume to tell you what to do, but if you'll read that sentence aloud, like you're talking to your great-grandmother in a wind tunnel, the next paragraph will be much funnier.)

And I'm almost sure our students asked one another in Polish, "Why did the Americans send a couple of deaf kids with learning disabilities to teach us to read? Don't we already get made fun of enough?"

But the Poles didn't need or want to be taught English. Their schools were doing a fine job of teaching foreign languages. No, our new Polish friends wanted to know about American sports. They wanted to be taught baseball. This was a potential problem. I'm not an exceptional athlete. In fact, "not an exceptional athlete" is a polite gym teacher way of saying that I'm awful at sports.

I learned at an early age that whenever I was forced to do anything physical like playing touch football with my friends or basketball in gym class or softball with a church group, I had to find a way to make myself feel better about myself. And so, even to this day, as my shot bounces ridiculously off of the rim or the football ricochets off of my face, I regularly have mental conversations with myself where I am encouraged by a mantra that helped me survive junior high:

"Bryan, you stink at this. But at least you're good at other things."

One day I hope to discover what those other things are.

So in an attempt to be culturally relevant, our new missionary strategy became to teach baseball so that we could teach then English so that we could teach Jesus. It was Wal-Mart Christianity at its finest. People come in for one thing and leave with four things that weren't on their lists. And we hope that Jesus doesn't get lost in the marketing. I wonder if the greatest story ever told really needs our help to make it more interesting.

Our first challenge was to find a baseball bat. Looking for an authentic baseball bat in Warsaw was like searching for swim goggles in the Sahara. The former Eastern Block Communist leaders didn't exactly encourage their Polish subservients to carry bats and clubs. I can't imagine why. When we finally found a bat, it was obvious that authentic baseballs were totally out of the question. So we used tennis balls.

After a brief sign-language explanation of the rules, including what I thought was a brilliant interpretive dance demonstrating how and when to run the bases, our first batter stepped up to the plate. His name was Bartek. And he was huge. Bartek looked like the Jolly Green Giant, only not so jolly and a little less green.

As he stood balancing the bat like a club, I asked "Bartek, are you ready?"

He responded with an unintelligible grunt that I assumed was Polish for, "Bring it on." My translation wasn't far off.

I started by tossing Bartek a Christmas present right over home plate. The pitch lobbed in a beautiful arc, slow and perfectly placed. This was my first mistake. I underestimated a worthy opponent. Bartek hit the tennis ball like I've never seen a ball hit. It soared out of sight, into the clouds, bounced off of the space shuttle, re-entered the Earth's atmosphere, and literally burst into flames. Seriously. It was unbelievable.

As the comet finally dropped back into the outfield, it fell straight toward a right fielder named Marek. Marek was a good guy. Eager. His eye was on the ball. And he had a big stupid grin on his face because he wanted to catch the ball. And I had a big stupid grin on my face because I wanted him to catch the ball. And he caught the ball. With his hands. I was so proud.

But just as Marek caught the ball, I saw from the corner of my eye that Bartek wasn't rounding the bases like my interpretive dance had clearly instructed him to do. Instead, he was running at full speed in a straight line toward the outfield. He was running directly at Marek who was still celebrating his tremendous catch, oblivious of his impending doom. His celebration was cut short as Bartek lunged at Marek, lowered his shoulder, and knocked him to the ground with a thud.

"No!" I yelled while waving my arms in a desperate pantomime. "Don't you know that baseball isn't a contact sport? You don't tackle the guy who catches the ball. You let him catch the ball if he can. Your job is to run around the bases. Just run around the bases. Do you understand?" Bartek grunted again, which could have meant one of two things. Either he understood what I was saying and was processing the information, or the sausage we had for lunch was doing to him exactly what it was doing to me. I wasn't sure which.

The next time I pitched the ball, I threw it with a little less arc and a little more heat. And again, Bartek smacked it. He knocked the Penn 6 completely off our tennis ball. It streaked into the air, breaking the speed of sound. The ball went so high that it had to radio back for clearance to land. By the time it returned to the outfield, the tennis ball was little more than a streak of screaming green fuzz. And Marek was right under it ready to make the catch.

Poor guy. He caught the ball. He actually caught the ball. Again. He should have learned his lesson and let it fall. But he didn't. Just as Marek wrapped his hands around the steaming tennis ball, Bartek began his charge. Head down, nostrils flared. The boy was a train. The impact of Bartek's massive body would have killed a lesser man. But not Marek. He took the hit like a champ. A champ who has just been hit by a train. When his body finally stopped bouncing, Marek looked up from his resting place with dirt in his teeth and said, "Me no like baseball."

Bartek disagreed. The only English words I would ever hear him speak were, "Me like baseball."

Bartek hit a homerun every time he stepped up to the plate, but he never ran the bases.

At least he's good at other things.

In his short but brilliant book *The Sacrament of the Present Moment*, eighteenth-century writer Jean-Pierre DeCaussade wrote, "There remains one single duty. It is to keep one's gaze fixed on the master one has chosen and to be constantly listening so as to understand and hear and immediately obey his will." [3]

For some reason, I generally take this to mean that running the bases and living a life of quiet obedience is not only less dramatic, but also less spiritual than racing with reckless abandon toward whatever grand plan God has for me in the future.*

Maybe the master wants me to drop everything and run. Maybe he wants me to lower my shoulder and charge blindly and faithfully into the future. Maybe I'm sitting right on the edge of a great life-changing plan and I just have to step into it. But how am I to know? How do I know where to move or when to change or what to do or who to choose?

After all, this life is the only one that I've lived. It's the only game I've played. The bases I'm running are worn and familiar. The sun rises and the sun sets and hurries around to rise again. The wind blows south and north, here and there, twisting back and forth, getting nowhere. The rivers run into the sea, but the sea is never full. Then the water returns again to the rivers and flows again to the sea. My day ends just as it began, and I seldom see God streaking out of heaven with a cry of, "Hey, guys, let's go this way!"

**This is not, however what DeCaussade would say. He would say that God's desire for all of us is nothing more than for us to be obedient in the present moment. He wrote, "You are seeking God, dear sister, and he is everywhere. Everything proclaims him to you, everything reveals him to you, everything brings him to you. He is by your side, over you, around and in you. Here is his dwelling and yet you still seek him. Ah! You are searching for God, the idea of God in his essential being. You seek perfection and it lies in everything that happens to you — your sufferings, your actions, your impulses are the mysteries under which God reveals himself to you."*[4]

So I look for purpose in the past and I find it. I remember happy times and wonder if I will be happy again. I remember work well done and wonder if I will work well again. I see where God has done great things for me in the past and hope that he will do something great for me again sometime soon. If I haven't peaked too early. If he hasn't already done for me whatever it is he has planned to do for me. And that makes me anxious. So I look to the future, which doesn't help.

My anxiety only grows because I feel like something great is always just in front of me, an inch out of my reach. And I worry about tomorrow because even though I want to run after God's plan, I don't know what that plan is. God has planted eternity in the human heart, but even so, people cannot see the whole scope of his work from beginning to end. How can I pursue something I can't see and don't understand? The wise men had a star to follow. Moses had a bush. Bartek had a tennis ball. What am I supposed to follow?

I want to live my spirituality with Bartek's passion and abandon. I want to charge fearlessly into the future. I want to believe that, like Frodo Baggins, I have volunteered for a grand adventure that is worthy of being immortalized in song and story and on a big screen. I want to see where God is, where he's working, how he's moving and chase him there. Something about that kind of passion feels attractive and right. But I sometimes get so anxious about what I think God may be doing in another place and at another time that I overlook and neglect what he's doing here. Now.

Maybe God isn't hiding in the future or camped out somewhere in the past. Maybe he's waiting for me in the present. Maybe now is the most sacred moment of all. Maybe doing

God's will is nothing more than being faithful with what's right in front of me.

After all, I cannot know the mind of God. I can't see the scope of his work from beginning to end. I can never really know if something was the will of God until I've done it. Only then can I look back and see how right and trustworthy his plan was. And so, now is the time to act. Not tomorrow. Today is the moment of my faithfulness.

In the Talmud, an ancient collection of Hebrew wisdom that reflects on the teaching of the Old Testament, the rabbis tell a story that goes like this:

"There was a pipe in the sanctuary which was smooth and thin, made of reeds from the days of Moses, and its sound was pleasant. The king ordered it overlaid with gold, and its sound was no longer pleasant. Then its overlay was removed and its sound was pleasant again as before.

"There was a cymbal in the sanctuary from the days of Moses, made of bronze and its sound was pleasant. It became damaged. The sages sent for craftsmen in Alexandria of Egypt and they repaired it, but its sound was not pleasant any more. Then they removed the improvement and its sound became as pleasant as before.

"The pool of Shiloah gushed forth through an opening the size of a coin. The king commanded that it be widened so that its waters would be increased, but its waters diminished. Then it was narrowed again, whereupon it had its original flow." [5]

Maybe my life doesn't need to be fixed as much as it needs to be enjoyed.

There is a time for everything, a season for every activity under heaven. … God has made everything beautiful for its own time. [6]

Maybe the game that I'm playing now, the bases I'm running now, the life I live now, the job I hold now, and the tasks that I find myself in now *are* the plan God has for me. That's not to say that there might not be something better for me in the future, but what if God wants nothing more than for me to be recklessly obedient now? What if God isn't as concerned about tomorrow as he is about today? What if his name isn't just "I Will Be" or "I Was"? What if I can know the God whose name is "I Am"? What if my relationship with this God isn't limited by the past or wrapped up in the future, but is to be enjoyed today?

I have a tendency to become so distracted by what I want for my life to be that I forget that my life as it is now is what God has given me. It is all of what God has given me. It's the job he has given me. It's the relationships he has given me. It's the responsibility he has given me. Maybe running the bases of my life isn't as sexy and exciting as I'd like it to be. But if I'm constantly looking toward what I hope God *will* do for me, I'm liable to miss what God is *already doing* for me. I think that's why Jesus said not to be anxious about tomorrow. If I constantly think that tomorrow will be better, then I won't see God today. And today is the game I've been given to play. Today is when he wants me to be the most faithful. Today is when he will be my joy, my peace, my forgiveness, my security, my instructor, my discipline, my hope, and my home.

But even as I look for the beauty of this moment, my eye will always be on the outfield. And I will always be ready to run.

Because eternity has been placed in my heart.

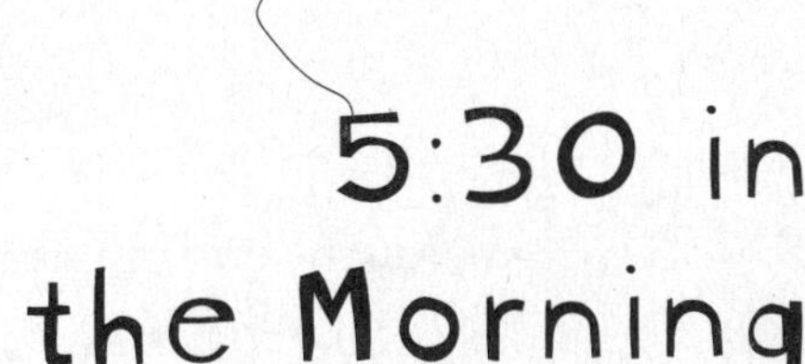

5:30 in the Morning

First of all, let me say that it was a restless night. It was one of those nights when you toss and turn and have crazy dreams about Batman and your third grade teacher. I don't know if it was a full moon or if I had Mexican for dinner or if my brain is an unpublished Steven King novel, but all was not well in my house.

Five-thirty in the morning rolled around, and it was still very dark outside. Of course, it seemed especially dark partly because my eyes were closed. My eyes are always closed at 5:30 a.m. I know most people get up early to go to school or work, but I'm done with school and I work at home, so there's nothing to be done at 5:30 in the morning that I can't do at 6:30 … or 7:30 … or noon.

So at 5:30 I was asleep, but it had been a rough night, so I was barely asleep when I heard a pounding at my door. Not a gentle knocking. A pounding. At 5:30 in the morning. You have to understand that my front door and my bedroom door are right next to each other. And since I'm single and I live by myself, I leave my bedroom door open. There is no denying that I heard a pounding. At 5:30. But at that hour it doesn't matter who you are or what you want, I don't care. Unless you are a member of my immediate family and you are on fire, I just don't care. And if you are a member of my family and you are on fire, you are probably not going to get in your car, drive to my house, and knock on my door to tell me about it. And even if you do, at 5:30 in the morning I don't care.

But I did care when I heard the whoosh of my front door opening. I cared even more when I heard three footsteps make their way into my front hall. I definitely heard a knock. But I'm certain I did not hear myself say, "Come in." Now all I could hear was the sound of blood pounding in my ears.

Somebody was in my house.

A bigger, stronger, braver man would have reacted. But I'm not bigger, stronger, or braver. My first instinct was to pull the covers up over my head and wet my pants. But that would probably not be the most manly thing to do. So I figured I had two options:

Option 1: Keep my eyes closed. Pretend to be asleep. When I did this as a child, my mom would tuck the covers up under my chin and kiss my forehead, and I would know that everything was right with the world. I wanted everything to be right with the world. But I did not want the intruder to kiss my forehead.

Option 2: Count to three, open my eyes, and potentially see the scariest thing of my life — some dude standing in my doorway with a machete.

Obviously, I could not just lie there pretending to be asleep while a stranger stole everything I owned. So I decided that I would count to three and open my eyes and wake up. But I was not only going to wake up, I was going to wake up with a vengeance. I was going to wake up, leap out of bed, and do something. I don't know exactly what I thought that something was going to be. All I knew was that my uninvited guest was about to have a half-naked thirty-year-old man with crazy bed hair and killer nasty morning breath all up in his mix. If that doesn't make you regret breaking into somebody's house, nothing will.

So I started my count to three. One … two … and just before I reached three, I heard the front door close. At this point I didn't know if this sound meant that the intruder had left or that he was committed to staying, but I was too far along in my countdown to back out. On three I jettisoned the covers and cleared the end of my bed like an Olympic athlete. It really must have been an amazing sight to see. I was Superman leaping over my Serta in a single bound. I don't know what I thought I was going to do once I got there, but it was going to be big. I was definitely going to knock this guy off his balanced breakfast.

But when I got to the door, there was nobody in the hall. Nobody to attack. Nobody waiting to attack me. But my front door was unlocked.

Someone had been in my house.

After the pounding of my heart got back to a normal rhythm, I analyzed the situation and deduced a couple of key things:

Realization 1: Thieves don't usually knock before they enter. That would defeat one of the main objectives of thievery. If they knock before they take your stuff, they're not stealing from you. They're evicting you.

Realization 2: Thieves don't usually rob at 5:30 in the morning when normal people are home and getting ready for work.

That's when the pieces began to fit together. Work. 5:30 in the morning. I live in a condo where all of the buildings and front doors look essentially the same. What if one of my neighbors had somebody coming by to pick him up for work? It's dark. The doors are practically identical. So the picker-upper knocks. No answer. He Pounds. Nobody comes to the door. "This is my friend," the person says to himself. "He's probably still in the bathroom or finishing a bowl of Lucky Charms. Hopefully he's not finishing a bowl of Lucky Charms in the bathroom. That would be weird. I'll just let myself in. He knows I'm coming. No big deal."

It's no big deal when you accidentally cut in line at the grocery store.

It's no big deal when you forget to turn your phone off at the movies.

It is a big deal when you walk into someone's house that you don't know and stand there and watch him sleep. It's a big, creepy deal. It's a big, creepy, prosecutable deal. It's a big, creepy, prosecutable deal that has seriously motivated me to invest in an actual pair of pajamas.

And to lock my front door.

But what if the stranger had been five seconds stupider? What if the intruder had paused for just a moment longer before realizing his terrible mistake? His day would have started off quite differently. He would have looked up from his coffee to see nothing but a blur of body and boxer shorts as I leapt on him like Charlie on a chocolate bar. I'm certain he would have spilled his half-caf, non-fat, extra-hot caramel macchiatto. Good morning, sunshine.

I know it was cowardly of me to hesitate before acting. But scientists tell us that this is perfectly normal. It's called the fight or flight syndrome. When faced with conflict, there is an instinctive pause where our brains decide whether it is wiser to fight or run like mad.

In that moment, the body gets prepared. The heart starts pumping at two to three times its normal speed, sending nutrient-rich blood to the major muscles in the arms and legs so they can either stand their ground or get out. The tiny capillaries under the surface of the skin close down so the body can sustain a surface wound and not bleed to death. This is why scared people look pale. The eyes dilate so they can see better. Hairs stand on end, making us more sensitive to our environment while making us appear larger, hopefully intimidating our opponent. All functions of the body not needed for the upcoming struggle shut down. Breathing speeds up to get more air into the system so the increased blood flow can be re-oxygenated. Fat from cells and glucose from the liver are metabolized to create instant energy. Sweat glands open, providing cooling for our over-worked system. If necessary, excess waste is eliminated to make us light on our feet (but unfortunately wet in the britches). Endorphins, the body's natural painkillers, are released. Just in case.

This is our body's way of saying, "Something big is going on here. What are you going to do about it?"

For those of us who are followers of Christ, we believe that something big is going on. We believe that God is real and at work in our world and in our lives. He hasn't invaded, but he has asked to come in. He knocked. And we answered. He woke us up from our sleepy lives.

I like to think of this God as my friend. I'm not afraid of him. He's my God big buddy. But I forget that he is a great deal more than that. He is omniscient, able to see all. I am not. He is omnipotent, all powerful. I am not. He is holy, pure and without fault. I am not. And when I, small little me, have a relationship with this big being, when this omniscient, omnipotent, all holy God interacts with me, it's inevitable that there is going to be conflict. Friction.

If not, something is wrong.

But when this friction comes, do I fight or do I flee? When God reminds me that he actually wants a living, breathing, working relationship with me, am I really ready for that kind of commitment? Am I ready to confront and be confronted by this God?

Selfishly, I want my faith to stay happy and fluffy and feel good like I'm God's Tickle-Me-Elmo. I want a YaYa Sisterhood approach to spirituality where everything is love and laughter and songs and acceptance and tears of joy (or so I've been told by friends who actually saw the film). But I wonder if that thought process has made me spiritually fat and lazy. I wonder if I am becoming a Christian junkie looking for his emotional fix. I wonder if I need to leap out of my comfortable Christianity and wrestle with God for a while.

I wonder if I need to be knocked off balance.

What if God has entered my life, not just to tell me that he loves me and to make me a nicer person, but because he wants to wrestle? What if he wants to wrestle with me about my sin? I may fight back sometimes because I like my sin. But I hope I'll care enough to actually wrestle and not just give up and give in. What if he wants to wrestle with me about my calling? I may roll around with him for a while.

As much as I want to be obedient, God's calling sometimes scares me to death. But at least when I wrestle I'm not just pulling the covers over my head. What if he wants to wrestle with me about my spiritual growth? He might get a fight with that one. Growth takes effort on my part, and I'm lazy. And sometimes it's easier to close my eyes and pretend to be asleep.

The question is, Will I fight or will I flee?

In the first half of the Bible, a man once wrestled with God. His name was Jacob. He didn't actually wrestle in the

Bible. There wouldn't be room for him in there. He wrestled with God on the banks of a river. We just read his story in the Bible. And in the story, Jacob and God wrestled all night. He wrestled with God all night and won. [1]

He actually won.

Either this Jacob guy was a hoss or God is a wimp. But I have learned that when this story took place, Jacob was ninety-seven years old. I don't care if milk has done your body good, at ninety-seven you're pretty much played out. And God is no wimp. Read the last book of the Bible. Wimp is not on the label of the can God opens.

I don't think the point of the wrestling match is that Jacob was strong. I think the point is that he was stubborn. He was willing to fight all night. Jacob's whole life had been spent fighting (and sometimes lying and cheating) to get what he wanted, and this time was going to be no different. He was willing to wrestle even with God. It is shamefully rare that I do much more than give God a quick hello a couple of times a day, much less actually spend the time it would take to wrestle.

I often sit in worship events and sing that I want him to "open the eyes of my heart," but how often do I open his word? And even when I do open it, do I actually wrestle with what's there? By two o'clock, the lessons I thought I learned have usually been flushed and forgotten with the tea I drank at lunch. I want to hear "the plans that he has for my life, plans to prosper me and not to harm me. Plans to give me a future with great hope," but I seldom wrestle with him in prayer. I talk a lot, but I don't listen. And when I do listen, I often ignore. I don't wrestle.

I want to understand the deep mysteries and have the hard questions make sense. But how often do I fight through answers I don't like or ideas I don't agree with? I tell my spiritual friends that I'm "struggling" with any number of ideas or problems, but am I actually struggling? Or am I just sitting passively in my life, labeling any number of questions or sins as "struggles" without actually wrestling through them? Am I stubbornly fighting to the other side, or am I too content and lazy for all that would require?

What does it mean for me to wrestle with God? I think it means that I will not sit lazily in my life. I will forget what is behind and press on toward what is ahead through digging into scripture. I will read God's word not because I think God is locked in the words of a book or because I imagine its pages hold magical secrets that answer all my questions and solve all my problems, but because the Bible tells me the story of God. And I can relate to a story. I can wrestle with a story.

I will ask questions about the deep things that I do not understand. I will approach God with confidence. I will have conversations that matter with other people. I will not be complacent, and I will not give up. I will press forward into new adventures that challenge my faith and increase my dependence. And when those adventures scare me to death or leave me feeling desperately uncertain, I will wrestle with the God who has brought me to that new place. I will feel his will grapple with mine and try to grow through the encounter. I will not let go.

In other words, I will let myself be challenged. I will let myself be threatened by God. I will let him challenge my small ways of thinking, my ungodly lifestyle, my fear of the future, my need to control, my loneliness, my prejudices and preconceived notions about other people and my world, and anything else that might separate me from him.

In short, I will let God pick a fight with me about anything he wants, and when he does I will not run away.

I am seriously impressed that Jacob actually fought. I am even more impressed that he fought all night. I probably would have given up or run away. But Jacob did fight, and God was proud of his diligence. He was so proud that he renamed Jacob "Israel," a name that means "One Who Wrestled with God." What an honor. What an award to be given. What an incredible badge to wear.

I'm becoming convinced that as a people — as a Christian community — we need to be known less as a people who don't drink and don't smoke and do wear certain T-shirts, listen to certain music, and have nice bumper sticker answers to all of life's big tough questions, and more as a people who wrestle with God. People who are in the trenches, hurt, confused, questioning, and searching, but still trying to hammer this thing out. Like Jacob, too stubborn to back down.

Wrestlers.

But Jacob's new name, Israel, had another meaning. It could also be translated "The God Who Wrestles with Man." This is the God who sits in the dirt and wrestles with dirty people. For centuries the Jewish people tried to re-translate this name another way because they couldn't handle the idea that a Holy God would lower himself to wrestle in the dirt with a man. It was too intimate. Maybe that's why the Jews couldn't accept Jesus as the Messiah. Jesus was God in the ring with his people getting dirty. But let's just let the word say what it says. God Wrestles.

This isn't a statement that a relationship with God is overly hard. There are times when I dance with my Father God in fields of grace. But there are also times when I wrestle with him by the river. The name Israel doesn't assert that I have to wrestle, struggle, fight, kick, and scream to get what I need from God. It just implies that my relationship is intimate. It's human. And real.

Genuine friends confront each other when there's a problem. Real relationships experience pain as they grow. People who care will tell you when your breath stinks and your zipper is open. Real friends fight with each other and still love each other. That's not to say the fight doesn't hurt and isn't scary. But in the end a good fight doesn't lessen the love. It strengthens the relationship.

I usually want for God to meet me on my own terms. I want him to hand me a relationship and walk away. I want him to give me love, peace, forgiveness, and whatever else makes me feel good, then leave me alone. Certainly don't wrestle with me. Don't make me think. Or struggle. But that isn't a relationship. A relationship is give and take.

The beautiful truth is that God wants to wrestle with me. He wants to engage me. It is in this wrestling that I form an actual relationship with him. He stays with me and struggles with me on my own level. He's willing to get down in the dirt. With me.

This name Israel is an invitation. God doesn't want — and

won't settle for — an easy, cheap, shallow relationship with me. He is no more satisfied with canned, generic, fast food faith than I am. He doesn't want shallow and surface any more than I do.

He wants to wrestle.

But this wrestling doesn't have to be antagonistic. I don't always wrestle because I'm mad. Sometimes I fight just because I want to feel something.

In the movie *Fight Club,* Tyler Durden (played by Brad Pitt) and Ed Norton's character start an organization of men that meet with the sole purpose of beating the snot out of each other. They're not enemies. They don't hate each other. They just want to feel something. The Fight Club starts one night when Brad Pitt and Ed Norton are in the parking lot of a bar after closing and Brad Pitt asks Ed Norton to hit him. They aren't arguing. Brad just wants to see what it feels like.

When Ed Norton asks, "Why should I hit you?" Brad Pitt responds, "Why? I've never been in a fight before. Have you? How can you know anything about yourself if you've never been in a fight? I don't want to die without any scars."

And then, when the fight is over, the two men sit on the curb and say, "We should do this again sometime."

They just want to feel something.

Continue to work out your salvation with fear and trembling, for it is God who words in you to will and to act according to his good purpose. [2]

Maybe we wrestle just to feel something. To prove that we care.

I don't want to die without any scars either.

Afterward

I performed my first wedding this year. It's a little nerve wracking when a couple asks you to be responsible for legally binding them together for life. I suggested they consider a nice pinky-swear. But the groom insisted on an actual wedding. I think he just wanted an excuse to eat cake.

My friend Ryan said that he and Jama wanted their wedding to be fun and funny. And as the minister, he wanted me to make that happen. He didn't want for me to just stand in a suit on a stage and sermonize and pronounce them husband and wife. He wanted the wedding to have personality. To be fun. And funny.

Ryan and I have been good friends for a while, so I felt the freedom to tell him that I thought his funny wedding idea might be a mistake. Actually, I told him that I thought his common sense might have leaked out in the shower. I was sure that Jama wanted her wedding to end with "I now pronounce you husband and wife," not "Live from New York, it's Saturday night!"

"Do you really think your wedding is the best time for funny stories and stand-up comedy?" I asked. "This isn't a day when people are supposed to be laughing at the goofy guy on stage, unless that goofy guy is you. You want them to laugh? Then faint or drop the ring or put a kick-me sign on your back. This is supposed to be a day when people are focused on you and Jama and the love you've committed to share. Not on your minister friend making silly comments. Don't you want your wedding to be a little more serious?"

"But Jama and I laugh with each other all the time," he said. "Why should our wedding day be any different?"

Good point. Maybe a person's wedding should imitate their love and life.

Still, I was nervous. I stand on stages a lot. No big deal. I stand on stages and try to make people laugh a lot. Also no big deal. I do not, however, often stand on a stage and try to get a laugh from the family and friends of a beautiful woman wearing a pristine white dress who is preparing to commit her entire life to the sweating man standing next to her.

But I'm always up for a challenge.

On an evening in mid-September, the bride and groom met at the altar and prepared to begin their lives together. Standing center stage, I had the best seat in the house. After her father had given his beautiful daughter to his soon-to-be son-in-law, I turned to Jama, who looked like a daydream, and commented on the excitement Adam had when he first looked at Eve.

"'At last!' Adam exclaimed. 'She is my own flesh and bone! My family! She will be called woman."

It's no wonder Adam used exclamation points. He had spent the last hundred years naming cows and kangaroos and living with gorillas in the mist. Who wouldn't be ready for a change?

But even though we know Adam was excited about his new friend, Genesis doesn't comment on Eve's first reaction. I reminded Jama, however, that Eve led an easier life than many modern wives.

Eve didn't have a mother-in-law.

Eve didn't have to leave the house on Super Bowl Sunday.

Eve didn't have to compete with an iPod for her husband's attention (Jama giggled. She knows how much Ryan loves his iPod).

Eve — at least in the beginning — didn't have to do laundry.

Of course, one of her sons did end up being quite a problem, but that's another story.

The wedding was fun and funny. And beautiful. And intimate. People laughed. They cried. They wished they could be as happy as the young couple lighting their unity candle.

Then came the big finish. The moment we had all been waiting for. Vows had been exchanged. Rings were on fingers. Only one thing remained. The kiss.

I didn't plan it, but in a moment of marriage brilliance I heard myself say, "I now declare that you are husband and wife. Ryan, you may now hug your bride."

Hug your bride.

There was a confused pause before Ryan laughed and kissed her anyway.

The nerve of some guys. They just don't do what they're told.

A wedding is a serious time. Important. It's a binding contract of love and commitment between two people. But just because there are tuxedos and dresses involved doesn't mean they can't laugh and love all at the same time. And it doesn't mean friends and family can't join in. If we're too solemn, we waste all the flowers and music and dancing.

God's love for us is also serious. Important. It's a binding contract of commitment between heaven and humanity. Sometimes it's even solemn. A man being tortured to the point of death for the sins of the world is a pretty serious business. The three days surrounding the crucifixion were pretty intense. Solemn. But I don't get the impression that on this side of the cross we are required, or even requested, to stay that way.

I think the angel's pronouncement of "He isn't here! He is risen, just like he said he would!" was an invitation to party. The angel spoke in exclamation points on purpose. The moment the stone rolled away, the weekend changed from a funeral march to a wedding reception. The groom returned for his bride. And our hearts are filled with flowers and music and dancing.

When we take ourselves too seriously, when we don't laugh and love, I'm afraid we waste the joy of an empty tomb.

Our lives are a wedding that unite us with Christ. He has publicly declared his unending love for us. For better. For worse. Through richer or poorer. In sickness and in health. To love and to cherish. And that's not an invitation to legalism. Or guilt. Or even religious duty. It's an invitation to stand at the altar and smile.

So embrace the joy that comes in a relationship with the living Christ. Pray with your eyes open. Sing. Dance. Pay attention to the world around you. Laugh. Learn. Listen as other people tell you their stories. And then share your own.

Because every life is a story God tells.

Notes

Postcards from Panama

1. 1 John 1:1-4, NLT. Scripture quotations marked (NLT) are taken from the Holy Bible, New Living Translation, copyright © 1996. Used by permission of Tyndale House Publishers, Inc., Wheaton, Illinois 60189. All rights reserved.
2. John 21:24-25, NLT.
3. Luke 13:11, Luke 15:8, Matthew 13:3, Matthew 21:33, Matthew 25:14, Luke 15:4.
4. Matthew 13:44.
5. Romans 1:20, NLT.
6. Frederick Buechner, Telling Secrets: A Memoir (Harper San Francisco: San Francisco, 1991), 3.
7. Hebrews 1:1-2, NLT.
7. John 1:14, NLT.

Toxicodendren Radicans

1. John 8:1-11. Scripture taken from the HOLY BIBLE, NEW INTERNATIONAL VERSION. Copyright © 1973, 1978, 1984 International Bible Society. Used by permission of Zondervan Bible Publishers.
2. Isaiah 40:26-27, NLT.
3. Isaiah 40:27-31, NLT.
4. Colossians 3:8-10, NLT.
5. Ephesians 4:22-24, NLT.

Hootie Hoo

1. 2 Corinthians 12:7-9, NLT.
2. Romans 7:24-25, NLT.
3. Romans 8:1-2, NLT.

Dead Bunnies

1. Colossians 1:19-20, NLT.
2. Matthew 5:6, NIV.
3. Colossians 1:21-22, NLT.

Uno

1. Ephesians 2:4-5, NLT.
2. Ephesians 2:8-9, NLT.
3. Romans 5:6-10, NLT.
4. Romans 5:7-8, NLT.

Kooter with a K

1. Romans 8:5-7, NLT.
2. Hebrews 12:1-2, NLT.

Sand and Balloons

1. Psalm 51:6, NIV and NLT (respectively).
2. Psalm 51:1-7, NLT.
3. Hebrews 4:12, NLT.

The Butterfly

1. Ecclesiastes 3:11, NLT.
2. Matthew 25:29, NLT.
3. Jean-Pierre DeCaussade, The Sacrament of the Present Moment (Harper San Francisco: San Francisco, 1981), 9. Translated by Kitty Muggeridge.
4. Jean-Pierre DeCaussade, The Sacrament of the Present Moment. 18.
5. Talmud, Arachin. Quoted in Ecclesiastes: Stories to Live By. Translated, edited, and compiled by Rabbi Joshua S. Sperka (Bloch Publishing: New York, 1972), 82-83.
6. Ecclesiastes 3:1,11, NLT.

5:30 in the Morning

1. Genesis 32:22-30.
2. Philippians 2:12-13, NIV.

Acknowledgements

Special thanks to Scott Lee, without whom the bunnies never would have died. Your talent and friendship are invaluable. To all the people who have lived and contributed to the stories in this book, thank you for making life an adventure – my sister Kathy, my mom, Jordan, Jeremy, two drunk spring breakers (I hope you're feeling better), Jars of Clay, B and Gran, Nemo, an uninvited guest (whoever you are), Scott, Jeff, the angry seal (sorry about the rock), Kyle, Julie, the Butterfly, Indiana Jones, Eric (shpeakin' dig!), Bartek, Marek, David Wilcox and his son Nathan, the hypnotist and all his friends, Ryan and Jama, Kooter (I hope your car got fixed), Greg, Stephen, "Laura," Pancho, Jonathan, Mike, the ice cream lady (I'm still bitter), Mel, Bethany, and little Bryan. And of course John and Lisa for making little Bryan and giving him such a cool name. Thanks to my family, who are more wonderful than I sometimes make them out to be. Thanks to John Highsmith, just because he's a brother with whom I've built many stories. I'm not sure why our adventures couldn't be translated into book form. Actually I am sure. Prosecution. A special shout to the Ninnies. If you don't know, it's just so much. And to our friends at the Buccaneer Resort, Panama, I have one suggestion. Wash your dog. Ryan Gregg, I owe you money. Thanks for your patience and encouragement in the process. Beth and Greg, thanks for all you did to get this project off the ground. Also, thanks to Braden and Gracie. Not because you're in the book or even able to read it yet, but because I think you're two of the coolest people on the planet. For all my other friends who wanted to see their names in print on the acknowledgement page, a very special thanks goes to (insert name here) ______________________.

And for B. Don't feel bad. Without your eyedropper and your good intentions, my book wouldn't have a title.